CHAMPION
HORSES AND PONIES

David & Charles' Equestrian Titles
Behaviour Problems in Horses · *Susan McBane*
Breeding and Training a Horse or Pony · *Ann Sutcliffe*
Champion Horses and Ponies · *Pamela Macgregor-Morris*
Compleat Horse · *Johannes E. Flade*
Dressage: Begin the Right Way · *Lockie Richards*
Equine Fitness · *Dr David Snow and Colin Vogel*
The Horse and the Law · *Donald Cassell*
Horse Breeding · *Peter Rossdale*
Horse Driving Trials: The Art of Competitive Coachmanship · *Tom Coombs*
The Horse's Health from A to Z · *Peter Rossdale and Susan M. Wreford*
The Horse Owner's Handbook · *Monty Mortimer*
The Imperial Horse: The Saga of the Lipizzaners · *Hans-Heinrich Isenbart and Emil M. Buhrer*
Keeping a Horse Outdoors · *Susan McBane*
Lungeing: The Horse and Rider · *Sheila Inderwick*
The Riding Instructor's Handbook · *Monty Mortimer*
Riding and Stable Safety · *Ann Brock*
Transporting your Horse or Pony · *Chris Larter and Tony Jackson*

CHAMPION HORSES AND PONIES

PAMELA MACGREGOR-MORRIS

DAVID & CHARLES
Newton Abbot   London   North Pomfret (Vt)

*Dedicated to the new professional showmen:
may they maintain the standards of their predecessors
in production and presentation, exhibiting benevolence in
defeat, magnanimity in victory, and manners as good as those
of their charges*

British Library Cataloguing in Publication Data

Macgregor-Morris, Pamela
  Champion horses and ponies.
  1. Show horses   2. Show ponies
  I. Title
  798.2'4   SF295.185

  ISBN 0-7153-9026-0

Typeset by Typesetters (Birmingham) Ltd Smethwick West Midlands
and printed in Great Britain
by Butler & Tanner Limited, Frome and London
for David & Charles Publishers plc
Brunel House   Newton Abbot   Devon

Published in the United States of America
by David & Charles Inc
North Pomfret   Vermont 05053   USA

CONTENTS

FOREWORD

My father Lord Knutsford wrote the foreword to the first 'Champion Horses and Ponies', which was published in 1956. Pamela Macgregor-Morris has asked me to do the same for this most splendidly written updated version. I feel very honoured to do so, and to follow in my father's footsteps.

In the original foreword a paragraph says, 'There is no doubt that really first class horses are hard to find, but when produced they still compare very favourably with the heroes of the past'. This still stands, but is even more relevant today.

In the days when horses of quality and up to weight could be found, they were bred from hunter mares of substance and Thoroughbred stallions. This must be the obvious way. The new method of using half-bred stallions is long term, hoping that the second generation will produce what is wanted – not an immediate result, but of course there are exceptions. It is sincerely hoped that some decent mares will result from this approach.

One wonders why anyone is surprised at the price asked for a good sort of horse, when one thinks of the problems and the vast expense involved in breeding horses. However, the changing face of the modern horse world, and the various types of horses required, leave those who only want horses to hunt in the minority. Therefore the old-fashioned top middleweight hunter is worth its weight in gold in 1987.

But how proud one is when one owns such a horse.

Diana Holland-Hibbert
Munden, 1988

INTRODUCTION
What is a Champion Horse or Pony?

There are three main ways of assessing a champion: by conformation and movement, as in the show-ring, for horses judged in-hand such as stallions, brood mares and young stock under 4 years old; by conformation, movement and ride, which also includes manners and training, for horses of 4 years or over; and by performance, or ability across country, over fences or in a race, a hunter trial, a show-jumping competition or a three-day event.

The cheapest way to acquire a champion is to breed one, unless one is fortunate enough, and a sufficiently good judge of a young horse, to buy one in the rough. The first essential is therefore a brood mare, preferably one who has been well hunted and proved herself in the field to be bold, capable of doing her three days a fortnight, sound and temperate, with a good temperament and a strong constitution. She should be deep and roomy, with well-sprung ribs, should stand over ground on good limbs with a preponderance of flat, flinty bone. She needs big knees and hocks, the former convex and the latter without the sickle front line that predisposes to curbs. The cannon-bones should be short, with well-defined tendons, the pasterns of medium length and gently sloping, and the feet open and of medium size, with well-developed frogs and concave soles.

The head should show great quality and intelligence, with well-pricked ears and large, generous eyes. The neck should be of medium length, well muscled with a convex crest and a concave underside – few things are worse than an upside-down neck because such a horse will never bridle or be really under control – running into a well-sloped shoulder, which will predispose the animal to be a good ride, even at a gallop downhill. It is said that a good shoulder is a luxury and a good hind leg a necessity, but I consider them both to be necessities, especially in a hilly part of the world.

The back should be strong and devoid of any slackness, running down from a well-defined wither over well-muscled loins to the croup. A tendency to goose-rump gives a mean appearance to the hind quarters and the tail should be set on high – 'at the top of his back', as the saying goes. Good length from the hip-bone to the point of the hock denotes galloping ability. The back-bone should not be too prominent. A good conformation can be illustrated by every photograph in this book far better than I can describe it, and it enables horses to continue in hard work until old age if they are never asked to do too much when unfit. Asking too much of a horse which is out of condition will break it down, and a horse that comes home overtired will lose condition rapidly and take a long time to recover.

It is a good practice to buy or breed a filly, break her when she is 3 years old and then turn her away for a year, having put her in foal. Thus she has a year to continue maturing, is at the same time usefully employed, and will breed more easily at the end of her working life if she has had a foal when young. Even if she is only to be retained as a brood mare, it is still wise to work her for a year in order to accustom her to the world at large and to make her more biddable than she would be were she to remain unridden.

The more bone that the mare has, the better foal she is going to breed, and there is no bone to approach that produced by the limestone belt that runs across the Irish Republic, through Limerick, Tipperary, Cork, Waterford, Kilkenny, Wexford, Wicklow and up into Meath and Kildare. It is hard, flat, flinty bone and it is to be found both in the Thoroughbred horse, the Irish Draught horse and the Connemara pony. Mares with a mixture of all three breed some wonderful hunters and cobs when put to Thoroughbred stallions, and although the show-jumping fraternity largely go shopping in the Netherlands and in Germany, the Dutch and German three-day event riders, as well as the Italians, Americans and Canadians, tend to buy their horses in England and Ireland.

The reason for this is not hard to seek. The British Isles, as the spiritual home of foxhunting, have for four centuries bred horses to follow hounds across country. Their preoccupation with hunting and racing led them to evolve the Thoroughbred horse, by importing three Arabian stallions – the Darley Arabian, the Godolphin Arabian and the Byerley Turk. Crossed with native mares, they produced the bloodlines which are still winning the top-class international classics from the Derby downwards. They also produced the steeplechaser, and they have been used all over the world to improve the national breed of riding horses. Great Britain, in effect, gave the world its best horses, in addition to the English language and the parliamentary system.

In modern times, largely owing to the premium stallions of the Hunters' Improvement and National Light Horse Breeding Society, the small breeder has been able to produce Grand National winners, world and European champions in the three-day event and in show-jumping, and Olympic gold medallists in both these disciplines. The HIS was founded in 1885, when, between 1873 and 1882, Britain imported the staggering number of 197,000 horses, at a cost of between £6 and £7 million. By encouraging farmers with the award of premiums to stand good, sound Thoroughbred stallions at stud throughout the British Isles to serve other farmers' mares at a small stud fee, the home supply was encouraged and increased by the War Office at a saving of millions of pounds.

In later years, first with the advent of the internal combustion engine and later with the mechanisation of the Army shortly before World War II, horses were relegated to the role of a pleasure animal and the emphasis has been placed increasingly on quality rather than quantity. Horses are no longer required on the roads to draw vehicles, although the combined driving competitions, based on the lines of the ridden three-day event, have given a new lease of life to such breeds as the Cleveland Bay, the Welsh cob and most of the nine breeds of British native pony. But, for all general purposes involving the better-than-average rider, the type of horse in the greatest demand is the middleweight hunter type, capable of carrying 14 stone and of following hounds across a good country and, because it should also be capable, with training, of performing in a three-day or one-day horse trial and in a novice show-jumping competition, known to the modern generation, in contemporary parlance, as a 'competition horse'.

Horses with the best conformation are, all else being equal in terms of courage and activity, the best performers; so the emphasis for selection must still be placed on a horse's make and shape, his quality and movement — on the standards of the show-ring, in fact. Horse-shows originated with the sole purpose of improving the breed, not only of the horse and pony, including all breeds of heavy horse, but also of cattle, sheep, pigs and any other type of animal one cares to name — although it is dubious whether dog-shows (and even foxhound-shows) have done a great deal to improve the animal. But in an animal where conformation and performance are so closely allied, human errors of judgement are relentlessly exposed.

The British Isles have a great strength in their horse-breeding enterprises, and that is in the variety and quality of their native mares. From the time when the first Thoroughbreds were bred, these foundation stock mares were active animals of the Yorkshire Coach Horse type (like a Cleveland Bay, with more substance), such as Black Bess, whom the highwayman Dick Turpin rode from London to York to establish an alibi. These mares naturally produced, to a Thoroughbred, progeny better than themselves, as did their offspring when put to an eastern stallion again. On the Continent, however, the only mares were of the cold-blooded, heavy Draught type like the Flemish or Ardennes breeds, and these could not compare for courage, activity or ability to gallop with British and Irish stock.

Between the wars several dealers in England – notably the late Victor Parry of Cheltenham – observing that the German horses looked the part, imported some of them to sell on as hunters. His son, Captain Brian Parry, explained:

> They were useless. No guts. After five minutes in the mud they were done – didn't want to know. In many ways they are very brave horses; look at their show-jumpers, going down to a massive wall, but when things go wrong they just die on you. I suppose they're basically soft, but all right if you don't want to gallop. People never buy them to win chases, or three-day events.

British Thoroughbred horses have been exported over the world for centuries, and so have horses of the British and Irish hunter type. Cleveland Bays have long been found in the United States, not only on their own merit but also as foundation stock for hunters, imparting bone and substance without loss of quality. Now British native ponies are carrying on the good work in Europe, the USA and the Antipodes, and it can be claimed unequivocally that British-bred ancestors predominate. For all of them, the testing ground over the years has been the hunting field. Long may it continue to be.

Even English cart-horses have proved a useful foundation for international show-jumpers of the highest class. Colonel Harry Llewellyn's great horse Foxhunter, who as well as being an Olympic gold medallist at Helsinki in 1952 was also a triple winner of the King George V Gold Cup, the most coveted grand prix in the world, was by the premium stallion Erehwemos out of a mare by Step Forward out of a Clydesdale mare. He started his life being hunted by a Leicestershire farmer, Harold Holmes, with the Belvoir hounds. One of his team mates in the winning Olympic team, Wilf White's Nizefela, who started life in a plough in his native Lincolnshire, had Shire blood on the distaff side and became one of the best Nations Cup horses in the world.

Colonel Alois Podajsky, commandant of the Spanish Riding School of Vienna, was very keen when he retired from this Mecca of the Lippizaner horse on the Thoroughbred-Welsh cob cross-bred. He bought several from Miss Ann Wheatcroft, who has a Welsh cob stud in Gloucestershire near Stow-on-the-Wold, and maintained that they could be taught anything and were excellent rides. For others, they might have too much knee action. I recall David Broome's father, Mr Fred Broome, enthusing over a cob he had bought at the Dublin Horse Show to take back to the principality. Would it not be taking coals to Newcastle, I queried? 'I can get the ones that bend their knees at home!' he replied. 'This fella doesn't – he's got Connemara pony and Irish Draught on his dam's side!'

HUNTERS · IN · HAND

THE PREMIUM STALLION

There are many advantages when selecting a premium stallion to serve one's mare, and the greatest is that the horse is warranted sound and free from hereditary disease, has not been tubed or hobdayed and is not parrot-mouthed (a lack of alignment between upper and lower jaws which renders grazing impossible). A fertility percentage of less than 50 the previous season debars it from exhibition at the stallion show.

Another reason for using a premium horse is that most of them have been in training, which is positive proof that it has stood up to the hurly-burly of racing and emerged from it intact. Premiums amount to £750 each, and in addition the top fourteen stallions win super premiums, which start at £660 for the champion and £630 to the runner-up, with £600 for the horse placed third, down to £360 for the fourteenth.

The horses are exhibited in six district classes, according to the part of the world in which they operate: 1, Dumfries and North Yorkshire; 2, Cambridgeshire, Derbyshire, Leicestershire, Northamptonshire, Nottinghamshire and Buckinghamshire; 3, Cheshire and Lancashire, Shropshire and North and Central Wales; 4, from Staffordshire down through the Cotswolds to Wiltshire; 5, from Lincolnshire and Norfolk to Essex and Hertfordshire down to Surrey, Sussex and Kent; 6, Berkshire, Hampshire and the West-country.

There is also a class for stallions new to the premium scheme which have not been out of training for more than two years, for the award of the Macdonald-Buchanan Cup. This class opens the judging at 9am, and as this is the class for the champions of the future, all the true enthusiasts make a point of being on the rails or in the stand when the horses are led in.

Plate 1 Max Abram with his triple winner of the King George V Cup, Current
Magic (Kit Houghton)

Typical of the best of these novice winners was Graham Lloyd's
Current Magic, who triumphed in 1978. His owner had bought him
at the Ascot sales for a mere 600 guineas, and he had stood up to five
years in training, from 1972. As a 2-year-old, he won once out of 6
starts, the Sandown Park Stakes over 5 furlongs. He ran 9 times as a
3-year-old, winning the Grand Stand Handicap over 7 furlongs at
Haydock and placing twice. Again starting 9 times at 4 years old, he
won the Eagle Handicap over 1½ miles at Warwick and was placed
5 times. At 5 he started 10 times, winning the Bowler Novices Hurdle
over 2 miles at Worcester and was placed 4 times. At the age of 6, out
of 9 starts, he won 3 times (the Albrighton Handicap Hurdle at
Wolverhampton over 2½ miles, the High Level Handicap Hurdle at
Wolverhampton and the Walrus Handicap Hurdle at Haydock over
the same distance).

A grand type of bay horse, 16.3hh, with beautiful limbs that will
stay sound forever, a lot of bone and marvellously convex knees,
Current Magic went on to win the King George V Cup the following
year, and again in 1982 and 1983. His greatest rival was Jimmy

Snell's Saunter, who stands in Cornwall and won in 1978 and 1981. By Current Coin, by Hook Money, out of Phosphorence by Aureole, grandam Steam Turbine, by Tehran, since 1982 he has left Herefordshire and become the property of Max Abram of Busk Hill Stud, Westow, Yorkshire.

The most successful exhibitor of premium stallions ever was Charlie Mumford, who lived at the Tea Caddy Stud in Northamptonshire and first showed a stallion at the Royal Agricultural Hall, Islington, at the age of 16 for his father, Stephen Mumford. He could remember travelling up to London on the train with his father and several stallions, joining other stallion men at different stations and alighting at King's Cross, where the Mannings, Mumfords and Hillmans proceeded to lead their stallions to the hall through the streets of North London. It was a hard week's work, but although they slept in a loose-box next to their horses, it was also a very social occasion and they looked forward to it from year to year.

Owners of premium stallions make little money – Max Abram reckons it is necessary to have six to make it pay at all, and six mares can make the difference between profit and loss – but the stallion owners are all dedicated enthusiasts and although their vocation could not be called a good living, it is certainly a good way of life. Jimmy Snell used to be a baker at Helston, but he soon gave up the bakery to keep stallions full time. He won the King's Cup with Brother in 1968 as well as Saunter in 1978 and 1981.

Bill Manning was also born to premium stallions, and his family, who had a brewery in Towcester, moved down to Wing, near Leighton Buzzard in the Whaddon Chase country, and farmed as well as breeding horses. He won the King George V Cup with Henry Tudor, an Irish horse who came from Jack Bamber of Ballymena, Co Antrim, in 1948 and 1949, with Erin's Pride in 1953 and with Border Legend in 1959 and 1960. Then he went out of the premium scheme, and stood top-class 'chasing stallions, which were more lucrative.

His head lad was John Rawding, now a highly successful stallion owner himself and a winner of the Macdonald-Buchanan Cup with Cartoonist (1967) and Legal Tender ten years later. But no one can approach the record of Charlie Mumford – War Star won the King's Cup in 1950, Court Nez in 1951, Cul-de-Sac (1952), Inchydoney (1954), Court Nez (1955), Your Fancy (1956), Starlata (1957), Parting Shot (1958), Bleep (1963–5), Quality Fair (1966 and 1969–72) and Royal Clipper (1976).

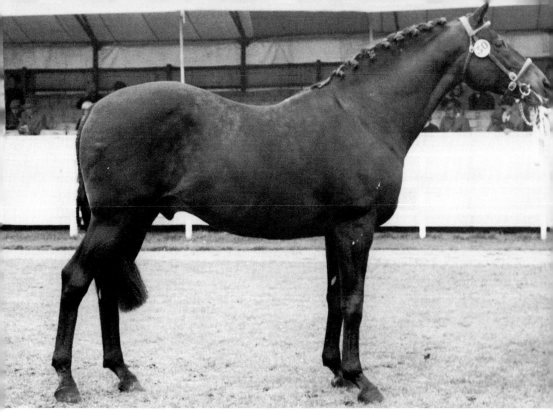

Plate 2 Kadir Cup, who was awarded eleven successive Premiums from 1962–72, and five Super Premiums (*National Light Horse Breeding Society*)

Oddly enough, although Quality Fair was champion on no fewer than six occasions, he never bred anything of note. In 1985, however, his son Fisherman, out of a champion heavyweight mare called Heron, won the championship at the Devon County Show, ridden and produced by Roy Trigg, who tells the story that Princess Anne, who presented the silver cup, asked him how Fisherman was bred. When he told her, she immediately lost interest.

In 1984, the centenary year of the HIS, the Queen honoured the society by becoming its president. At Newmarket in March she presented her grandfather's cup to a new exhibitor, Louis Massarella from Leicestershire, for his bay Barley Hill, winner of the Macdonald-Buchanan Cup for the best young horse two years earlier. Foaled in 1976, he is by Simbir, by Shantung, out of Pixie Hill, by Goldhill, and won three races, at Newmarket and Ascot, as a 3-year-old and two handicaps at Ascot at the age of 4.

Mr Massarella was a newcomer to the world of premium stallions, although his cousins are well known in the show-jumping world. They are the offspring of two brothers from southern Italy, near Naples, who set off to seek their fortunes in the United States between the wars and eventually decided to settle down in Doncaster, England, where they made ice-cream which they sold from hand-carts and later pony-carts. Thus they became connected with horses, and started jumping at local gymkhanas. Their business prospered and eventually was bought by Joseph Lyons (of Corner House fame), although they subsequently bought it back again. Their best horse, Mister Softee, they bought in Dublin and he became a triple European champion, ridden by David Barker and David Broome (twice).

The story goes that once they bought a show-jumper for £600 soon after World War II and paid for it with three of the big, old-fashioned square biscuit tins, full of sixpences and three-penny bits – the proceeds of a large number of ice-cream cones. The hapless seller had to sit down and count it all – and was not pleased to discover that the total was 6s 9d short!

Although it is unarguable that British-bred event horses are the best, the show-jumping fraternity and the dressage queens favour the so-called Warmbloods which Germany and the Netherlands produce so successfully for these purposes.

One of the earliest importers of Hanoverian horses, some thirty years ago, was the Hon Mrs Edward Kidd, daughter of the late Lord Beaverbrook, who founded the *Daily Express* and the *Evening Standard*. Under the prefix Maple, in deference to her Canadian ancestry, Janet Kidd stood a succession of stallions at stud, first near Milverton in Somerset and later in Surrey. Their progeny, especially of Maple Duel, show-jumped with both her children and did dressage with her daughter Jane. Now there are half-a-dozen Hanoverian studs in Britain, as well as a couple of Trakehner studs and one for Holsteins.

Jennie Loriston-Clarke (née Bullen) was the first to popularise the Dutch Warmblood in England when she imported Dutch Courage, who was as successful in the dressage arena as he was at stud, finishing highly placed in the World Championship Grand Prix and carrying off the bronze medal at Goodwood. This was no mean feat, having trained the horse herself. Britain's leading international dressage horse for six years, he is now renowned as a sire of top-class international competition horses, including Dutch Gold, who stands with him at the Catherston Stud, Brockenhurst, in the New Forest, and not only is an advanced international dressage horse but won the Novice Horse Trials Championships at Locko Park in 1983;

Catherston Dutch Auction (he won three three-day events in Germany) and Catherston Dutch Bid (an outstanding winner in 1985 of four National Dressage Championships, the Open Spillers at the Horse of the Year Show and Working Hunter Championship at the Royal Show).

The late Caroline Bradley was also an enthusiast of the Dutch Warmblood, having won top international competitions, including the Queen Elizabeth II Cup at the Royal International Horse Show at Wembley on John Harding's entire Marius, who divided his time between the international show-jumping circuit and his stud duties. Caroline also had great success with the grey Hanoverian, Tigre, a horse who had been rejected as unridable by such experts as the German team rider Gerd Wiltfang and most of the German team. But with Caroline he was a reformed character, helping to win for Britain the World Team Championship at Aachen in 1978 and the European Championship a year later.

Scotland's John Brown and his father Alec also favour the Dutch Warmblood, and have stood Odion at Muirmill for seven years. Their compatriot, Susan Fichtner (née Irving), and her German husband Gerhard have brought a graded and tested Bavarian Warmblood, Duplikat, to stand at her family estate, Straloch, near Newmacher, Aberdeenshire, and two more in Ayrshire and in Fife. The enterprise is sponsored by the Bavarian State Breeding Society.

James Aird is jumping the Holstein stallions Calgary and Foreign Affair for Mr and Mrs David McWilliam of Balfron, Stirlingshire. Foreign Affair stood for one season with Max Abram in Yorkshire on lease, when the Whitakers were among those who took a mare to him, and his 4-year-olds made a good impression in Yorkshire in 1986.

The British Warmblood Society have inaugurated the British Sports Horse Register so that foals can be recorded similar to those bred by Mrs Doreen Wilson of Cumbernauld, Glasgow's Summerhill Stud. Her stallion, which she hopes will breed her a top dressage horse, is Flying Dutchman, by Dutch Courage out of the TB intermediate eventer/show-jumper Wild Laughter. Seven years old with 9in of bone and standing 16.3hh, he is also show-jumped by James Aird. Among his patrons are many aspiring breeders of event horses.

Some of the best show-jumpers in the world have traditionally come from Ireland, as well as the best hunters and show-jumpers, and there is no shortage of Irish Draught stallions in England as well as Ireland to put bone and substance back into stock that has become too fine to withstand the rough and tumble of the hunting field. After one outcross to Irish Draught, the resulting fillies can return to Thoroughbred sires again and the influence will continue for generations, especially if the land grows bone.

The most successful sires of hunters have been of medium height – from 15.3 to 16.1 hands – and thick-set, muscular and short-legged. They must be teeming with masculine character, full of courage and nervous energy, and of an equable temperament. Cottage, that great sire of hunters and 'chasers including Grand National and Gold Cup winners, was a veritable man-eater, and some of his progeny were funny-tempered, but he was the exception that proves the rule.

The nearest thing to a British Warmblood stallion is the Cleveland Bay, but this separate and distinguished breed, which has been the pride of Yorkshire since medieval times, merits a chapter to itself to do justice to its history.

THE HUNTER BROOD MARE

It is a traditional saying among breeders that temperament comes from the sire and constitution from the dam. In fact, it has long been recognised that the dam is every bit as important as the sire, if not more so. The best brood mares are often the smaller ones, from 15.1 to 16hh and they usually produce big, robust foals, whereas the 17-hand mare often brings forth rabbits, for some reason. Although she does not need to be tall to produce big stock, she does require to be deep and roomy, and she is permitted to be longer in the back than a stallion or gelding is allowed to be for this very reason.

The mares that have produced the best hunters – animals of strength and substance, with at least 8in of bone below the knee, which is what carries weight – have usually been hunter-bred themselves, by a Thoroughbred horse out of a mare who is at most three-quarters Thoroughbred so that she can bestow some plebian blood to her progeny. Many of these types of mares, however, were destroyed during the war, when they were shipped from Ireland in their hundreds to the abattoirs of Amsterdam. When the war was over, everyone was keen to breed a point-to-point horse, so the true hunter mare became rarer and rarer, both on the farms and in the show-ring.

This is not to say that all Thoroughbred horses lack bone or weight-carrying capacity – far from it. Prince Regent, a great and gallant horse who was one of the best never to win the Grand National because he was consistently weighted out of it with an imposition of 13 stone to carry, was a model of a heavyweight hunter – the sort of horse that is seldom bred and when he is commands a very high price to go steeplechasing. The blood horse up to 14–15 stone has always been, and will always be, worth anything his owner cares to ask for him.

An old-fashioned top-class hunter-bred mare is indeed a pearl beyond price. She will have quality and substance, straight and true all-round action, and her conformation will be as nearly perfect as possible, for all too often she will transmit the worst of her faults and few of her virtues to her progeny. The limbs in particular must be as good as may be, free from disposition to curbs, not tied in below the knee or – horror of all horrors – back of the knee, or they will certainly break down with work. Plenty of flat, flinty bone below the knee is essential for wearing qualities, and the fetlock joints must be clean and cool, the pasterns sloping and of medium length for a springy ride. She must be deep and rangy, and height is no criterion of anything, while a narrow mare with close-set hips and flat ribs is never a good brood mare. As long as she stands over ground and is big within her own compass she will produce foals that will dwarf her at maturity.

The first outstanding mare to come out after the last war was Mr Ian Scott's Travel Alone, by Jilted, dam Lady Member by Political. Bred by Mr Harry Lewis of Usk, she was sold as a foal for £15 in 1935, Mr Scott having owned her grandam, Flannelette. Travel Alone first won at the Shropshire and West Midlands as a 2-year-old, also at the Three Counties, Peterborough and the Royal Welsh. A year later she won at the Royal and was then sold with another the same age as her owner was overstocked. She soon expressed her disapproval and her new owners could do nothing with her, so she went back to her birthplace.

The war interfered with her riding career and when she reappeared it was as a matron in the heavyweight division. She was never beaten, winning with five foals at the Hunter Show, the Royal and Peterborough. After slipping twins she never really picked up and was put down in 1954.

She was followed on by Mrs M. H. Tollit's Seaward II, foaled in

Plate 3 Mrs M. H. Tollit's Seaward II, Champion Brood Mare

Plate 4 Prince's Grace, winner in 1965 at the National Hunter Show of the HIS Challenge Cup for the Best Hunter Brood Mare

1940, by Merely-a-Minor out of the hunter mare Shagreen II, by Grenoble. She was bred in Gloucestershire by Mrs T. F. R. Bulkeley who, having put her dam in foal, then went off to serve for three years with the Free French. Seaward II won lightweight and working hunter classes in her youth and, ridden by Miss Kit Tatham-Warter, won and was placed in seventeen point-to-points. Mrs Tollit bought her in 1952, and the next year she came out as a matron, beating Mr Norman Crow's Irish-bred chestnut May Marcus, by Lord Marcus, ex a mare by Little Marten. Foaled in 1941, she was a consistent winner at the Royal, Peterborough, the Hunter Show, Three Counties and Great Yorkshire. Champion at the Hunter Show in 1951, she usually had to give best to Seaward in a championship.

With Seaforth, Seamyth and a colt by Archive at foot, Seaward II, all of whose foals were destined to be winners in the ring, is one of only two mares since the last world war to have won the HIS Champion Challenge Cup for the best brood mare on three occasions, and the only one to have won it in three successive years – 1954–6. The other was Mrs A. L. Wood's Prince's Grace – a mare, incidentally, who was also once the property of Natalie Tollit. She was legendary, for she was equally successful under saddle as she was in hand.

Mrs Tollit found her when she was staying with 'Gino' Henson, for many years Master of the Blankney, for the Lincolnshire Show.

Jimmy [Disney, her now octogenarian stud groom, and a famous character] warned me not to be late as Herbert Sutton was judging, but all the level-crossing gates seemed to be shut and I was not early. I finished about eighth with my yearling, but it didn't matter because in the next class I saw the most lovely 2-year-old filly ever coming into the ring. Herbert Sutton put her fourth and I thought there must be something wrong; a Shire chap was showing her, who told me the boss wasn't there, he'd gone racing. He was Rex Chappell, the owner of Prince's Game, her sire. She'd run twice and I saw him at Newmarket and I bought both her and her dam, Collence, the dam of the Australian Olympic three-day-event gold medallist, Laurie Morgan's good hunter 'chaser, College Master.

Harry Bonner rode PG for me before I bought her, she was coming 5, looked awful and Harry wasn't at all keen on her, but I got one glimpse of what she could do and be and I had to have her. Hugh Sumner saw her finish second at the Three Counties, and when she won at Cambridge he came over to me and bought her for Jean Wood, his daughter. She was tremendously successful under both saddles, often winning the championship from Hugh's heavyweight, the Dublin champion Work of Art. Then she had just as much success in the ring as a brood mare – though oddly enough she never bred anything of much merit, either showing or racing, though Jean sent her to much better stallions than I should have done.

Perhaps the reason was that, beautiful though Grace undoubtedly was, she never had the look of a horse that is listening.

The heavyweight hunter brood mare is becoming increasingly hard to find, especially if it has the quality to go with its bone and substance. Years ago in Ireland they used to keep some of the good 'chasing mares out of the Stud Book to win bona fide races, and these made wonderful matrons when their racing life was over. Now the weight-carrying mare is generally bred by accident rather than design, although they are certainly more plentiful in Ireland than anywhere else. Here, however, it should be noted that many of the modern Irish Draught-type mares tend to be very back of their knees and these should be eschewed at all costs.

Mr Geoffrey Palmer (of the Huntley & Palmer biscuit firm at Reading) devoted the last half of his life to breeding weight-carrying hunters. He and Major Kenneth Wallis travelled over to Celle and bought some half-dozen Holstein fillies and generously presented them to the Hunters' Improvement Society in the hope that they would make hunter brood mares. Alas, they did not. The older they got, the more common they grew – a presentable yearling would become a monstrously plebeian 4-year-old, so the experiment was costly and abortive.

Geoffrey Palmer's next foray was to Ballsbridge for the Royal Dublin Society's Horse Show, where he was much more successful, finding a wonderful mare called Killowen Lace, by Interlace, belonging to a worthy called Paddy Carty. He liked her and he liked the foal she had at foot; but her owner resisted every blandishment to part with her. It was several years before he succeeded in taking her across the pond, but at long last he succeeded, and in triumph he changed her name to Formula, although everyone now knew her as Carty's Mare. Not only did she breed him some good offspring, she also emerged as champion mare in 1961 and again in 1966.

Mr Roly Harker, longtime Master of the Jed Forest in the Scottish Borders, had the champion heavyweight mare at Shrewsbury in 1969 and 1970 – Dunkery, whose son Morning Glory, by Barbin, did well for Roy Trigg and then, still in his ownership, became a useful show-jumper with Derek Ricketts. Another useful mare who went from the

Plate 5 Mr and Mrs Norman Skinner's Ocean Cheer (by Three Cheers out of Eastern Ocean), who won over hurdles, and her daughter Kon Tiki, Champion Foal at the National Hunter Show in 1970 when her mother won the matron's class, and Champion Filly at the Hunter Show and the Royal in 1971. Another daughter, Three Wishes, won the Lloyds Bank qualifier at the 1977 Royal Highland, and then the final at the Horse of the Year Show for Mr and Mrs Andrew McCowan as a 3-year-old

Plate 6 Hon Mrs R. N. Crossley's Supreme Champion of the breeding classes at the Newark & Notts Show in 1982: her home-bred Cuillin Hills (Carol Gilson)

hunting field to stud was Mrs S. C. Lloyd's Cathy Garnette, named after her breeder Mrs Garnet, who was well known in the North Cornwall country, riding side-saddle. By Little Cloud (by Nimbus out of Little Britain, by Epigram), her dam was the Irish mare Limerick, by Foroughi. Cathy Garnette was champion heavyweight in 1975 and 1977, emerging supreme in the latter year.

Another much-garlanded matron is the Hon Mrs R. N. Crossley's Cuillin Hills, by Count Albany out of the Irish Draught half-bred mare Loch Ness, by that great sire of jumpers, Water Serpent. Colonel Crossley hunted the Middleton Hounds off her in her youth, and when she went to stud, as she only breeds every other year (Archie Thomlinson's Ancient Monro is the only stallion who can get her in foal, moreover), he continued to hunt hounds off her during her off years.

Mr and Mrs Reg Burrington's Heron, who won the heavyweight cup at the Hunter Show from 1981 to 1983 and was supreme on the first occasion, was bred in Leicestershire by Major Tim Hellyer (by

Comandeer out of Linnet VII), who sold her as a brood mare after her successful career as a filly, which might not have continued under saddle in view of her somewhat upright shoulders. She did exceptionally well as a matron, until she had the misfortune to die of colic in 1985.

After all these heavyweight mares, the record ends with perhaps the most remarkable Hunter Show champion, Douglas Kellow's little 15.2hh grey charmer, Shalbourne Honeymoon. Bred by Miss Marguerite de Beaumont near Marlborough, she gave her to Mr Kellow, who had produced so many of her ponies and hacks with his family from their home on Bodmin Moor. She was by the Thoroughbred polo pony Clieveden Boy, by Ujiji out of Fair Road by Fairway. Foaled in 1946, Clieveden Boy ran for two seasons under Pony Turf Club Rules, winning five times, and was registered as a polo pony. He won at the Royal from 1953 to 1955, the National Pony show in 1954–5 and the Ponies of Britain Stallion Show. In 1955 he was the champion polo pony stallion. He also sired eleven champions and a winner on the Flat, April Star, out of Noble Woman by the Cesarewitch winner Noble Star.

Shalbourne Honeymoon's dam was Honeysuckle VI, the champion hack of 1952, by the Arab stallion Basa Shagya, owned by the Dutch-born dressage expert Henry Wynmalen, who wrote the pre-war *Country Life* book, *Equitation*. Honeysuckle was out of June XI, a grey mare by the TB Gare de Falaise out of a French Anglo-Arab mare. Given as a foal to the late Mrs Noel Edwards, she bred six foals during the war and in 1946 was produced by Count Robert Orssich to become champion hack at Windsor, Richmond and the International. Unbeaten that year, she was later bought by Miss de Beaumont who, as her six foals had all been by TB sires and had grown into big horses, although Honeysuckle herself stood only 14.2½hh, sent her to the celebrated Hungarian-bred Arab. It speaks volumes for her dominant genes that neither Honeysuckle nor her children were Araby. Honeysuckle followed in her dam's footsteps by winning the Richmond, Windsor and International hack championships before being acclaimed Show Hack of the Year at Harringay, ridden by Count Orssich.

The best foal ever to have won the Hunter Show Championship was, to my mind, Ian Thomas's Lucky Fool, by Mandamus out of Lucky Strike, who was champion filly here for the late Mrs Molly Cail in 1973 and also won the Edward, Prince of Wales Cup for the

Plate 7 Ian Thomas's Champion Foal Lucky Fool, by Mandamus out of Lucky Strike (Kit Houghton)

champion young horse. I believe she was the first filly so to do, although she was emulated ten years later by Mrs Harry Hindle's and Miss A. Riddiough's Bright and Fair. By Lucky Leprechaun out of Falls of Bruar by Blandace, and bred at Castle Milk, Lockerbie by I. C. Watson, Lucky Strike was left to Ian Thomas, MVO, the Queen's dressmaker, when Mrs Cail died. She has bred a number of good young horses and Lucky Fool, who has a white foreleg from the ground to below the knee, inherits it from a paternal ancestor, through Petition and Fair Trial, to Spearmint, who won the Derby in 1906 and had the self-same stocking and star.

THE YOUNG HUNTER

The young horse judges are usually of a certain age – and not only because they are probably past riding a fit young horse in the show-ring, but because they have more experience of young horses, of the order in which they should place their priorities, and of how a youngster can alter in its make and shape from youth to maturity. There is no doubt that the young stock judges have, by and large, the hardest task of all who officiate in the show-ring. They must be almost clairvoyant, able not only to put what they see before them in the correct order of merit, to the best of their ability, but also to be capable of gazing into a crystal ball to envisage the raw-boned or overfat youngster that stands gawkily before them as the finished article it will be at 6 years old.

Young horses can alter in the most astonishing way. The fine big yearling may, as they say in Ireland, 'grow into quality' as he gets older; he may also, as a 4-year-old, develop into a common big brute. Combining Thoroughbred blood with cold blood, as it is known on the Continent, or cart-horse blood, is always fraught with hazard. It can go very wrong and it can also prove to be an excellent cross, combining the best of both worlds. Full brothers and sisters, moreover, can each encapsulate the worst and the best aspects of both parents, for in haphazard breeding of this sort nothing is certain. All breeding is a gamble, even when like is mated with like. When it is not, anything can happen, and often does. As a general rule, it can be accepted that the further away (by which I mean back in the pedigree) the alien blood lies, the better. Arab blood, for instance, produced the Thoroughbred, but it has not been repeated, and it would be disastrous if it were to be used again now. Similarly, at least two removes from Irish Draught are essential to produce a champion show horse. As for Clydesdale, Shire or Suffolk blood, at least three removes are essential in the first two instances, and I have yet to see a nice horse with Suffolk antecedents.

At the turn of the century a horse called Grudon won what was known, for obvious reasons, as the Snowstorm Grand National. His feet were packed with butter to prevent the snow balling in them, and the strategy paid dividends. Grudon had a sister who would not breed, and as she was a valuable mare, as a full sister to the winner of the world's greatest steeplechase in 1902, she was eventually turned out with a Shire colt, who duly worked the oracle and got her in foal.

This bloodline has gone on producing heavyweight horses to this day, for it is still possessed by Maxie Jones of the Elton Estate, near Peterborough. Fair Spark, by Quality Fair, won several championships, including the Three Counties for Norman Crow, the former Master of the North Shropshire, in 1974 (I believe it was on this occasion that someone remarked: 'Oh dear, poor things – they'll have to get another grand piano to take all the cups!').

Another relation was the South Essex Insurance Group's chestnut Assurance, by Crawter. Sold into Cornwall as a young horse, Vin Toulson saw him as a 4-year-old at the Horse of the Year Show in 1979 and was so captivated by his bone and movement that he was determined to buy him. Assurance won his first championship at Hertfordshire as a 5-year-old, also at the South of England and Great Northern shows, and was reserve champion at Windsor, Devon County and Bath & West. The following year he was runner-up for the Waterford Glass points championship he had won the previous year.

It is strange how many young horses who have a star-studded career in the young stock classes, winning every sort of championship imaginable at the leading shows, are never heard of again once they have outgrown the led category. Very few go on to win as 4-year-olds under saddle, and the reason for this is not far to seek. It does a young horse good to be shown a few times, perhaps on three or four occasions – say, at the local country show, at the Hunter Show, the Royal and at Peterborough, if he or she is good enough to aspire so high. It accustoms the youngster to people and horses en masse, teaches it manners and a taste of sophistication with its mother's reassuring companionship, which does it a world of good.

But the foal, and even more the young horse, is nowhere better off than at home in its field. Taken about incessantly hither and thither, it becomes like a precocious child that is allowed to stay up too late at night, while the constant travelling about in horse-boxes is positively detrimental. The legs are constantly braced to withstand the movement, which does the joints no good at all, and if rubber mats are put down to prevent them slipping, the effect is even worse, for they hold the feet still and put even more strain on the joints.

Some years ago Jack Stevens, an old friend who had farmed in Oxfordshire and retired down to Exmoor, was judging young stock at the Royal. When he had finished he came and talked to me as I sat on a chair in front of the Governors' stand. 'Well, what did I do wrong?' he asked, with a cheery grin.

He was far too sound a judge to do anything wrong, but one thing had perplexed me. There was a very nice bay 3-year-old that had been at virtually every show I had been to since the Bath & West in May – the Three Counties, the Hunter Show – and he had pulled it in second but then put it right out of the ribbons. I asked him why.

He's a very big colt. And he's been shown too much – he's got very big joints. I asked the fellow what he'd been doing with him, and pointed out that the horse had big joints. He looked at me pityingly. 'He needs big joints!' he said indignantly. 'He's a very big horse!'

What the owner did not know was that the youngster had big puffy joints from all the travelling and the hard going, as if he had done a lot of work. I recalled Betty Gingell, Master of the Cambridgeshire Harriers, telling me when she put him up at the Three Counties that she had advised him to turn the colt out and forget showing him or he would ruin that good young horse – which is exactly what he had done. The Irish, who have much more horse-sense than we, confine their best colts to a local show, Cork, Clonmel and Dublin. They do go on, given that sort of start in life. Roy Trigg, who has been producing show horses with great success all his life, won the 4-year-old class at the Royal in 1986 with a lovely chestnut heavyweight by Slippered that he bought at Cork for John Dunlop, the Arundel trainer, who loves a good horse. In the same year he bought a good 3-year-old that won at Cork from Captain Fergie Sutherland, a bay middleweight, who will doubtless in time take the place of Fisherman, the 14-stone horse by Royal Charger out of Heron with whom he has been so successful.

The hunter-bred colt who has been very successful in-hand can often become coarse as he approaches maturity, a contributory cause to their failure to fulfil early promise into the ridden classes, which does not affect the blood colt to anything like the same degree. I remember a breeder and trainer of bloodstock whom I met at the World Three-Day Event Championship in Lexington, Kentucky, in 1978 – his mother-in-law and I had sat together on the plane from New York. Accustomed as he was to magnificent Thoroughbreds – Secretariat, Sir Ivor and Nijinsky, among other equine giants, were just down the road at Claiborne – he could not get over the plebeian type of horses which so many of the three-day event horses seemed to be. 'Do they *have* to look like that to be eventers?' he demanded.

Thoroughbreds, of course, seldom lose their quality, but as far as his movement is concerned, the led horse can only be judged on his walk and trot. There is an old and true saying to the effect that a good walker, with a long, swinging, purposeful stride, is a good horse, and if he puts his toe out at the trot and moves as if on springs, that will also go in his favour if he moves straight. His galloping potential cannot be assessed, but a good shoulder, freely used, great length from the hip to the hocks and a long, easy stride indicate a latent ability to gallop, although they are not infallible, and a few in-hand champions have reappeared under saddle to confound their erstwhile admirers with the realisation that they cannot gallop fast enough to keep themselves warm.

Some young horses used to be kept as in a forcing house, fed on boiled barley so that they grew so fat it was impossible to see their frame, and generally kept stabled and denied a natural development. Mercifully, this treatment and fashion has become obsolete. In Ireland most young horses are shown more in store condition so they grow into value.

Bill Manning, who has bred a great many good horses, was told by his father that if one sees a foal before it has dried off after being born, it will eventually return to the same shape and conformation – and he has proved this to be true. This also indicates how very rapidly foals alter. They are unquestionably exceedingly difficult to judge, which is why a winning foal is often the biggest, best grown – or simply the oldest – in the class. Apart from the set of the shoulder, which does not change, or the proportionate length from hip to hock, almost nothing else remains constant. Hind legs can alter out of all recognition, and many good judges give them a year to go on improving. Some foals are born right down on their pasterns and take time for the fetlock joint to right itself, but with increasing strength it is miraculous how the ugly duckling develops into a swan. Movement is among the most difficult things to assess in a foal, who is generally bounding along at a canter after its mother, bucking and plunging, and disporting itself with the abandonment of youth rather than emulating its dam's sedate trot.

Judge Wylie, the benevolent dictator of the Dublin Horse Show for so many years, used to say that it was impossible to judge a foal – all you could do was look for two good ends and hope that one day they would join up! With the yearling it is a little easier, and the older a youngster becomes the more hopeful the judge can be of making a fairly accurate prognosis as to the way it will go. Ranginess is imperative, rather than a stuffy type, so evenly developed from head to tail that he looks fully mature while still a yearling, and has no room left to grow in any direction.

Perhaps the most deceptive single point in the young horse is the shoulder, which can appear to be a great deal better than it actually

32

Plate 8 Richard Burke's Fort Devon, by Fortina, who was the best exhibitor-bred young horse at the Dublin Horse Show in 1969. He grew to 17.2hh (Fiona Forbes)

appears to be when the saddle is put in place, as many purchasers of an in-hand champion have found to their cost. A straight shoulder is an abomination and purgatory to sit behind in a hilly country, especially when galloping downhill, when one becomes all too well aware how easy it would be to leave the ship by the front door.

Mr Harry Frank was one of the leading breeders and exhibitors of young stock between the wars, first in Yorkshire and then at Quelfurlong, near Malmesbury in the Duke of Beaufort's country. He had a wonderful mare called Alice Brownthorn, a TB by Loch Lomond out of Alice Whitethorn. Her son, Sam Brownthorn, was raced by Mr Harry Freeman-Jackson, Master of the Duhallow and former captain of the Irish three-day event team. Then there was Gay Donald, bred by Mr Frank in 1946 to win the Cheltenham Gold Cup in 1955. Out of Pas de Quatre, he was by Gay Light, holder of the course record at Lingfield. One of the best show colts to come out of Quelfurlong was the bay Glenarouske, bred well enough to win at

Aintree and champion at the Royal and at Peterborough at 2 years old and at Peterborough again at the age of 3. By Nearco's son Nearcolein out of Iceberg's Pride by Iceberg, he too went to Harry Freeman-Jackson in Co Cork.

Norman Crow made it a practice to annex a great many young stock classes and championships at the leading shows from his farm near Wellington, Shropshire, from 1952 until 1976, with the help of his wife Lena and a wonderful stud groom called Harry Jarrett, who was not only a very fine judge of a horse but adept at producing them and showing them in-hand. Year after year, the team of led horses, later reinforced by ridden champions, won at shows of the calibre of the neighbouring National Hunter Show, the Royal, Peterborough, the Great Yorkshire and many of the county shows, while the ridden horses also went to the Horse of the Year Show at Harringay and at Wembley.

Norman is descended from a family of weavers in Perth, whose three sons were sent to England with a new suit of clothes, a bible, their train fare and a golden sovereign, and bidden to make their fortunes on the land. As soon as they earned their fare they sent it back again, and all three young men finished up farming cheek by jowl in Shropshire. Norman also became Master of the North Shropshire Hounds in 1963 and retained them until 1975, returning from 1980 to 1983.

He started showing young horses, one of the best of which was Devotion, by Sea Lover, bought from Thomas Keating at the Ballsbridge sales. He won the Edward, Prince of Wales Cup at Shrewsbury on ten occasions with nine horses, and his wonderful middleweight, Top Notch by Top Walk, was champion at the Royal and Leading Hunter of the Year at Wembley, as well he deserved to be. He was also a great performer in the hunting field, which is worth a hundredfold more than all the other plaudits.

One of the very few youngsters to go on from a successful career in-hand to do even better under saddle was Mrs Tollit's brown filly Silverin, foaled in 1952, by Erin's Pride out of Silvereen by Silver Fox. She started by winning at the Royal as a yearling; as a 2-year-old she won at a dozen shows and took 5 championships; at 3 she won 14 out of 17 shows and took 6 supreme awards, including Peterborough, and was champion filly at the Royal. After winning under saddle with Harry Bonner in 1956, she was sold to the United States.

RIDDEN · HUNTERS

HEAVYWEIGHT

The true heavyweight show horse, a blood hunter that can carry 15 stone and upwards, consisting of man, saddle and both their accoutrements to hounds in the first flight for half a day, has never been easy to find and is now as rare as a good deed in a wicked world. There are still plenty of big horses with bone and substance about, but a large percentage of them are common brutes bearing a strong resemblance to the Suffolk Punch – badly balanced, round in their action, unable to gallop, with loaded shoulders that make them roll in their trot and flounder in their faster paces; the sort of horse, in fact, who is palpably incapable of carrying more than his own bulk through heavy going, without the added burden of a heavy rider. This type of animal is seldom seen in the hunting field, for he is anathema to the rider with any pretensions to being with hounds, but he is sometimes seen in the show-ring, trimmed and clipped within an inch of his life, and more often in the jumping arena, for common horses can often jump.

The quality heavyweight, on the other hand, is the embodiment of equine virtue, possessing a majesty and magnificence that proclaim him the monarch of the show-ring. Where the common horse is ponderous in movement, he moves with lightness and dignity. His trot may not be as spectacular as that of a lightweight, but his gallop eats up the ground and one can imagine him at the top of a good hunt when hounds are really running, while his courage stems from his breeding and it is unimaginable that he would turn his head. The underbred horse, if it gallops at all will shake the ground like an earthquake, but when the quality horse gallops past the stand there is never a tremor. Furthermore, his quality will help him to remain sound in wind and limb, which are subject to greater demands than in the lighter animal.

The main reason for the scarcity of quality heavyweights is the rarity of heavyweight brood mares to produce them. They must have a certain amount of cold, or cart blood, but it needs to be several generations back. A first cross between a Thoroughbred and a Draught mare will produce a common horse in 99 cases out of 100, although a Clydesdale mare may well be the great-grandam of a quality horse. The clean-legged Irish Draught mare, who is so active that she herself could be hunted, or the Cleveland Bay, are better foundation stock for the same reasons. But only the real enthusiast perseveres today with trying to breed weight-carrying hunters, for breeding non-Thoroughbred horses is one of the greatest gambles known to man. Full brothers can vary by over a hand in height, and the breeding of Thoroughbreds is not only safer but far more remunerative.

Between the wars many quality weight-carrying horses were bred in Yorkshire, utilising the native Cleveland, and Wales was also a happy hunting ground for the dealers, in that part of West Wales, Pembrokeshire and Carmarthenshire, which is known as 'the little England beyond Wales'. Here the tough blood hunters probably owed much of their stamina to the hardy, sure-footed Welsh cob. It was from Ireland, however, that the heavyweights came in the greatest numbers, bred on the farms in their dozens, usually by an old 'chasing sire that was often owned by a farmer or a vet and used by all his neighbours, out of those grand old Irish hunter mares, nearly clean bred, but just not in the Book (like the Grand National winners Lovely Cottage and Sheila's Cottage) which have now disappeared, more's the pity. No one seemed to know how they were bred in the tail female and no one particularly cared, for they were patently bred 'right'. They were the real sort, and 't'auld mare' might have ten or twelve offspring who acquitted themselves with distinction in the hunting field across the water, or in the show-ring.

If a likely purchaser insisted on a pedigree at one of the fairs like Ballinasloe or Buttevant or Cahirmee (all now gone), one might be written out on the back of a tattered old envelope — at one time they were all by Cottage, then Steel Point, later Knight's Wax, now Carnival Knight is the boy — they were all good horses, and what's in a name? However they were bred, a king might have been proud to ride any of them.

Nat Galway-Greer, the legendary dealer from Dunboyne, Co Meath, was a past master at finding Dublin Horse Show supreme champions; altogether he produced ten, and half of them were heavy-weights, while one, Prudent Lover, was a beautiful Thoroughbred. He was sold to the United States where he perished in a barn fire along with sixteen others, to the deep distress of Nat, who said he was the best horse he had ever owned, while Jack Gittins, who had won the title on him, described him as the best he had ever ridden. A bay 4-year-old by Gypse out of a mare by Power Cut, he was bought by Davey Harvey, Nat's best spotter, at the Meeting of the Waters in the Wicklow Mountains as a yearling, rising 2, for £500. Nat sold him on the telephone to an American woman for £7,500. He told me:

> He was in training with Paddy Sleator, and Paddy told me he could win over 3 furlongs or 3 miles – it was all the same to him. His new owner kept him to look at and as a trainer's hack for a year, and then he went on to win two Maryland Hunt Cups before he died in that fire – it must have been a terrible sight.

Nat's first champion, Mighty Fine, a liver chestnut heavyweight by Al Quaim out of a mare by Duke of Sparta, was bred in Co Cork by Mr Patrick Ball and foaled in 1941. His owner showed him at Cork as a 6-year-old, then Mr Galway-Greer bought him and took him to Dublin, where he won the heavyweight cup and the supreme championship. He was sold to Reg Hindley, who was in the cotton world in Lancashire and became captain of the British Olympic three-day event team in 1952.

In 1949 Mighty Fine won nine championships, including the Hunter Show, Peterborough, White City, Richmond and the Royal, and ended up by winning the Show Hunter of the Year title at Harringay. He won seven titles the following year, including the Gold Cup at Peterborough and the championship at the Royal for the second year running. But he failed to stay sound and this was his last year in the show-ring – he was never beaten in his class and only once in a championship, at Richmond by Ballykeane from Count Robert Orssich's stable, who won the novice class and the title and was never seen again.

Mighty Atom, also a liver chestnut, was Nat Galway-Greer's second Dublin champion. Foaled in 1944, by Rockminster by Rocksavage, he too was first produced in the ring by Paddy Ball, at Clonmel. Nat bought him and took him to Dublin in 1948 where he stood supreme. He was then bought by Mr W. H. (Horace) Cooper,

Plate 9 Mr W. H. Cooper's Mighty Atom, king of the ring for four seasons after winning the Dublin Supreme Championship (W. W. Rouch & Co)

who owned, in Beau Geste and Wavering Bee, some of the best show horses in England at his home near Hagley, Worcestershire.

The Atom was shown in England first in 1949, as a 5-year-old who had not quite grown to himself and needed another year. He never beat Mighty Fine and usually wound up reserve to him. By 1950 he had the stage to himself; he had grown into quality and was indomitable. Which was the better is a moot point, but it must be remembered that Mighty Fine, at 7, was a mature horse when he first appeared in England. Mighty Atom was at one time slightly cow-hocked, but when he had strengthened up he was very hard to fault, more powerful and better balanced in his gallop.

His first big win was the Royal Counties championship in 1949, and he was to win this title six times in all, with the Bath & West and City of Bath championships five times each and the HIS, Richmond, Royal and City of Birmingham four times each. He was also a quadruple Royal International champion and twice won the

Winston Churchill Cup for the supreme champion riding horse. He was a dual winner of the gold cup at Peterborough, the Harringay Hunter title and the Royal Windsor championship. Suffice it to summarise, he was monarch of all he surveyed and well deserved to be – a unique horse, successful with Harry Tatlow, Jim Daly and Roy Lester. He spent his retirement in a field overlooked by his owners' house, with a donkey as companion and friend.

When he retired in 1955, Mighty Atom's place was taken by Mr Bernard Selby's brown 6-year-old, His Grand Excellency, by Colare out of a mare by Ambassador. He won the championship at Cork as a 4-year-old for Tim Hyde, the brilliant steeplechase jockey who partnered the legendary Prince Regent in his races, and won the 1938 Grand National on Workman, besides riding the show-jumper Hack On. It was in a jumping competition that the unfortunate Tim broke his back over the double bank at Clonakilty Show, which confined him to a wheelchair ever after.

His Grand Excellency was bought by Mr Selby at Cork and bypassed Dublin for Sussex, where his new owner, who had owned several champion hunters before the war, had a big string of horses. As a 5-year-old, HGE was only moderately successful, but in 1955 he stood supreme at the Royal International, Royal Windsor and Richmond Royal – all 'London' shows as opposed to the real hunter shows like the Hunter Show, the Royal and Peterborough. But his turn came to prove himself at the genuine hunter shows too, when Mr F. G. Starling, an East Anglian farmer, bought him and asked Mrs Hugh Gingell, Master of the Cambridgeshire Harriers, to ride him. Then he crossed the country in pursuit of hounds all winter, paraded hounds at shows in the summer and did the lot – a wonderful life for a grand sort of horse, whose portrait by Richard Dupont hangs in a place of honour on Hugh and Betty's drawing-room wall.

The next notable heavyweight – another Irishman – was bay Work of Art, by Soldado out of a mare by King Cob, who was 6 when Jack Gittins won his first Dublin championship for Nat Galway-Greer in 1957. He was bought by Mr Hugh Sumner, Master of the Worcestershire Hounds and the chairman of Typhoo Tea, and although Captain Lionel Dawson, Hunting Correspondent to *The Daily Telegraph*, persistently referred to him as the Dray Horse (though not in print), he ruled the roost in the heavyweight division and was seldom beaten in a championship, save, perversely, by Mr

Plate 10 Roy Trigg on Mr R. H. Bonnett's Admiral, by Nordlys; the best heavyweight to come out of Dublin (Leslie Lane)

Sumner's daughter, Mrs Alex Wood, on her lightweight and ladies' side-saddle winner, Prince's Grace.

A few years ago, Captain E. Glen Browne, a former Master of the United in Co Cork, asked me at Ballsbridge, home of the Royal Dublin Society Horse Show: 'Which was the best heavyweight you have ever seen here?'

I pondered before replying: 'Mighty Atom, I suppose.'

'He wasn't, you know,' was his response.

'Who then?' I countered.

'Admiral,' he announced, 'without any shadow of doubt.'

Admiral was a horse who came down from the North of Ireland in the charge of the brothers McEvoy from Co Down. By that good sire Nordlys (also the sire of Mrs Elsie Morgan's of the West Waterford Gone Away, of whom more anon) he was a wild 5-year-old in 1970, and his attendants were pretty wild too, so much so that the horse had become very nappy. He failed to win the championship, but was reserve to a middleweight called The Yank, owned by Mr Tom

Moore, Master of the County Down Staghounds. He was then bought by Mr and Mrs R. A. Bonnett from Kent, and sent to Roy Trigg to produce. Roy spends his winters breaking yearlings before they go into training for the flat, for people like Lavinia, Duchess of Norfolk, and Captain Ryan Price, and he is a past master with difficult horses, but Admiral took so much time and patience that he could not be produced with confidence in the ring until more than a year after his appearance at Dublin, at the British Timken Show in late August. He won the championship there and ended the season by winning the Show Hunter of the Year title at Wembley from Norman Crow's middleweight son of Quality Fair, Fair Gin.

Even then his troubles were far from over. He missed Royal Windsor and made his first appearance in 1972 at the Bath & West, where Dick Francis, the former steeplechase jockey turned author of racing who-dunnits, put him only fifth in the heavyweight class – a decision that caused a considerable fluttering in the dovecotes, even though it is accepted that his judgements are often, to say the least of it, unpredictable.

A week later he came into his own at the South of England Show, where he stood supreme. 'The cough' caused his absence from the Royal, but Wembley proved a lucky arena for him both at the Royal International, and at the Horse of the Year Show, where he confirmed the form with Fair Gin on each occasion, successfully defending his title at the latter fixture. He scored predominantly on being a rare pattern of quality heavyweight and on his light and airy movement, and the way he covered the ground in his gallop. His sire Nordlys, who, like so many unfashionable (in terms of racing) Irish stallions, was not really appreciated for his full worth until he was an old horse, was also the sire of two Italian international show-jumpers – the winner of the 1972 individual gold medallist at Munich in 1972, Graziano Mancinelli's Ambassador, and Captain Raimondo d'Inzeo's Gone Away, who won the middleweight cup in Dublin when Mrs Morgan owned him. I saw him win the coveted Grand Prix in Rome in the most appalling conditions of teeming, unremitting rain and deep, holding going. Raimondo remarked afterwards: 'He loved it – he thought he was back in Ireland!'

Once at Hickstead it was thought to be a novel idea if Raimondo and Gone Away were to compete in the middleweight hunter class, which he could still have won. Raimondo looked doubtful but agreed to have a go some weeks before. However, when the time arrived he backed out. 'I couldn't bear to see the judges riding him!' he admitted.

Lady Zinnia Pollock (as she was then, though now, widowed when John Pollock incurred a fatal heart attack, she is Lady Zinnia Judd) competed with the professionals on equal terms when she built up a team of show hunters which often beat their combined efforts. She inherited her love of horses, and hunters in particular, from both her parents, the Earl and Countess of Londesborough, who were joint-Masters of the Blankney in Lincolnshire between the wars. This propensity was encouraged and nurtured by that brilliant horseman and showman, Jack Gittins, when she was 17 and used to stay with him in Leicestershire.

Two of the best horses she showed were heavyweights. Balmoral, by Game Rights, was found in the hunting field in the Scottish Borders. Beau Brummell, a son of the Duke of Northumberland's premium stallion Hamood, was sold from Lord Inchcape's hunting stable because he was so big. Each made his mark in the ring, as did Douglas Bunn's Selsey Bill, by Sunny Light, who had one very successful season in England in 1974 and won Peterborough's coveted Gold Cup, shown by Jack Gittins, but was bedevilled by the hard going the following year.

There is nothing to touch the Thoroughbred heavyweight horse, of course, and the best I have ever seen was Mr R. Appleyard's State Visit, bred by Mr and Mrs Christopher Marler in the Cotswolds, by the premium stallion Quadrangle out of Narrow Margin. He was a glorious horse, a real hunter with limbs and depth and his gallop was poetry in motion. Ridden by Jack Gittins, he won the novice class at the Oxfordshire Show at the start of the season and again at Northampton, but during the winter he got out of his field on to the main Oxford road and collided with a Mini, which left one forearm badly scarred. When he had recovered he was sold into Yorkshire to a market gardener called Mr Appleyard, who engaged a nagsman called Willie Hope to ride him.

State Visit galloped away with the championship at the Great Yorkshire for two successive seasons, 1967–8, and was eventually adjudged Show Hunter of the Year at Wembley after his owner had been tempted to show him more extensively by moving him to David Tatlow's yard in the Cotswolds. Alas, he ran up very light on a show a week, and was sold to go eventing. Not long after he was put down with navicular disease – a tragic end to a beautiful horse.

Plate 11 Willie Hope on State Visit, the Thoroughbred heavyweight who was supreme at the Great Yorkshire in 1967 and 1968, and took the Show Hunter of the Year title

The other successful Thoroughbred horse to win numerous heavyweight classes and championships was a failed racehorse, who was registered in the General Stud Book as Passing Light, an Irish-bred brown gelding by the good 'chasing sire, Black Tarquin out of Flipper by Flamenco, another 'chasing stallion. A failed racehorse, Passing Light ran his last race at Huntingdon in mid-March, ridden by Paul Blacker, finishing a bad fourth.

Vin Toulson has always thought him a horse with enormous show-ring potential and had been trying to buy him for eighteen months. Now the time seemed ripe: 'I knew his connections had backed him heavily and I anticipated that in their disappointment they would have lost confidence in him. I bid them £2,000 and he was mine.' He brought him out in June at the South of England Show after changing his name to Prince's Street, and Captain Brian Fanshawe (now

43

Master of the Cottesmore, and previously of the Galway Blazers and the Warwickshire), put him top of the novices and reserve to Admiral, the champion – who never beat him again.

The next week he stood champion at the Three Counties Show at Malvern, judged by Major George Rich; John Daniell put him over Fair Gin at Lincoln and David Nicholson did the same at Royal Norfolk; at the Royal Mike Gibson put him up in the novice class and then, under Colonel Stephen Eve, he won the heavyweight class from Admiral and went on to stand supreme. At Peterborough he beat Admiral again under Major John Howie, and finally, under the late 'Gino' Henson and Olympic three-day event gold medallist Bertie Hill, he won at Wembley the 1973 Show Hunter of the Year title.

I asked Major John Howie, who judged both State Visit and Prince's Street, which was the best. 'There is no comparison – State Visit, every time – but then he was quite exceptional, I should think the best horse I have ever ridden, though this horse is outstanding, too.'

But I was given food for thought in August when I arrived in Dublin, and Nat Galway-Greer chided me.

> I was surprised to see you writing up that failed racehorse *as a hunter*. Before the war one could buy them for £200, but I never did because they were useless. Remember always, it isn't the flying machine that gets to the end of the hunt, but the horse that can jump whatever he finds in front of him and go the shortest way!

He was right, of course, as he always was, and I was duly chastened – but, flat-catcher or not, Prince's Street did fill the eye, and I loved looking at him.

The 1983 Dublin champion, Edward Cash's Standing Ovation, was produced by Robert Oliver in 1985 to win the Show Hunter of the Year title at Wembley for Mr and Mrs Trevithick. By Carnival Knight, he went wrong in his wind, as so many big horses do, early in the 1986 season and his place as the Show Hunter of the Year was taken by Mrs Jane Dewer's Seabrooke, another chestnut, bred in Pembrokeshire and by 'Dewi' Lewis' former premium stallion, Stetchworth Lad, out of an Irish Draught-type mare. Stetchworth Lad stood only one season in England and is now standing in Ireland at Thomas O'Neill's Slyguff Stud, where the Irish Draught stallion King of Diamonds also stands, near Bagenalstown, Co Carlow.

Seabrooke was bred by Morris Eynon of Cresselly.

The 1986 Dublin champion, who was also supreme at Cork, was also produced by Mrs Frances Cash – the brown heavyweight Overture, another of Carnival Knight's get. Bred by the Queen, he stands in Mallow, Co Cork. Robert Oliver bought Overture before he won the supreme award, and sold him on to the Continent without ever bringing him home. Half-brother to eight winners, including Highclere, Tammuz and Carnival Knight, he is by Crepello (by Donnatello II) out of Highlight by Borealis.

MIDDLEWEIGHT

The true middleweight is a 14-stone horse, and in the best hunting countries that remain in England today – the Shires, the Cotswolds and from North Yorkshire to Northumberland – they are in the greatest demand as the horse to carry the average man. Although the shortage of good heavyweights is reflected to some extent in a corresponding dearth of quality middleweights, there are still many of the right sort being bred on both sides of the Irish Sea. Many are Thoroughbred, more are a trifle hard to place on the distaff side, but the common middleweight is seldom seen.

In the show-ring a really good middleweight will beat a moderate heavyweight in a championship, and a really outstanding 14-stone horse has been known to stand above a top-notch heavyweight as well.

The greatest middleweight to come out after the last war was Mr W. H. Cooper's Beau Geste, a bay gelding, 16.2hh, by Tagman by Craig-an-Eran out of Diana XVIII by The Alder. Foaled in 1939, he was bred in Shropshire by Mr E. H. Croft, who always had good brood mares about. His Melanie II won the HIS Champion Brood Mare Cup in 1952, and Yvonne (only marginally over 15hh) produced three champions – Romeo V, who was twice Show Hunter of the Year with Bill Bryan in the saddle for Mrs P. Morris, Brockton, and Dawn Chorus of Mrs Sugden's, who was champion foal at Shrewsbury in 1961 and, after a highly successful career, as an in-hand filly, became a much-garlanded matron.

Beau Geste was hunted with the South Shropshire by his breeder for three seasons and then sold to Mr Cooper, who had him produced in the ring by Harry Gittins at the Herefordshire Show. Later he was shown by Harry Tatlow. His first major victory was the

championship at Royal Windsor in 1946, which he won three times. He also won the Gold Cup at Peterborough twice, was twice champion at Richmond and Aldershot and three times at Bath.

An equally famous contemporary was Mr Hugh Sumner's Blarney Stone, a brown gelding foaled in 1942, by Praetor, by Phalaris out of a mare by Denis d'Or, by Tredennis. Bought late in 1945 from Mr N. D. Mahoney of Blarney, Co Cork, Mr Sumner showed him himself in his early career, winning at the Shropshire and West Midlands. The following year he stood champion at the Hunter Show, and in 1948 was supreme at the Oxfordshire and Royal shows. His best season was in 1949 when he retained his title at Oxford and reserve at the Hunter Show and at Peterborough and won his class at the Royal. After two years' absence from the ring, he staged a comeback in 1952, beating Mighty Atom in the Great Yorkshire championship and winning the Gold Cup at Peterborough, where the Atom did not oppose him.

During the majority of his show career he was ridden by J. H. Gittins of Severn Stoke, Worcestershire. A tremendous galloper, full of courage and joie de vivre, his very keenness made him difficult to ride. His owner showed hunters for more than forty years, starting with Loyalist I, by Lembirch, who was unbeaten as a 4-year-old in 1936, his victories including the Royal and Peterborough. Mr Sumner also had a number of good 'chasers in training, and sometimes observed that he preferred the certainty of being first past the post to the uncertainty of the show-ring.

The late William Hanson, whose father Robert was Master of the Grove and Rufford, had a good horse called Unique. By Match, by Hurry On, out of a mare by Ceylonese, he was bred in Co Wexford in 1944 by Mr Peter Somers, was third at Dublin for Nat Galway-Greer and was bought by E. P. Mills. As a 4-year-old he was champion at the Hunter Show, Peterborough and City of Oxford and was sold to Mr Hanson, who won the Harringay award for the most consistent hunter of the year. In 1951, his last and best season, he was champion at Newark and the Royal Lancs, and reserve at Windsor, Richmond, the Hunter Show, the Royal, the Great

Plate 12 Mr W. H. Cooper's Beau Geste, by Tagman, with H. Tatlow up

Plate 13 Mr J. R. Hugh Sumner's classic 14 stone horse Blarney Stone (1942) by Praetor (by Phalaris), dam by Denis d'Or (by Tredennis)

Yorkshire and Bath. He retired to carry the huntsman of the Grove and Rufford.

Mr Ronnie Marmont's Rajah III had, for a show horse, an unusual start to his career, for he ran promisingly over hurdles at Cheltenham in his youth, and when he was 7 won the Hunt race at the North Warwickshire point-to-point. His show career started later that same year (1947) when he won at the Hunt Show. By Gough's Auction, by General Gough out of Cottage Belle, a famous mare bred in Co Cork by Mrs Dorothy Browne of Glanmire, he was bred in Hertfordshire by Brig Sir Geoffrey Church. As a yearling he was bought by Miss Mary Haggie, and in 1949 he won the novice class at the Royal and at the White City. The following year at the Bath & West he divided Blarney Stone and Beau Geste and went on to win his first two ladies' classes, which were to prove a triumphant medium for him, at the Three Counties and the Hunter Show. He was then bought by Ronnie Marmont after repeating these successes at the Great Yorkshire. Soon afterwards, ridden by Mrs Bea Haggas, he won the Schweppes Cup at the Royal International. At Harringay he was the most consistent hunter of the year and in 1951 he was never beaten in ladies' classes. At Harringay he was again the most consistent hunter of the year and also won the working hunter class for good measure. In 1952 he was equally consistent in ladies' and middle-weight classes and at Harringay he won the Show Hunter of the Year title. In 1953 he won the Working Hunter title again and retired to the hunting field in Leicestershire.

The Hon Mrs James Baird testified to his sterling character. Once, when she was judging him at the Great Yorkshire, the side-saddle came around to rest beneath his tummy at full gallop, but he stopped instantly of his own accord, averting what could have been a perilous situation.

Then there was Earmark, owned by Mr Hugh Haldin and produced from Count Robert Orssich's stable near Windsor. A bay Thoroughbred, foaled in 1946, by Cariff out of Okehampton, he was bred in Ireland by Baron de Robeck and bought by Harry Bonner as a potential 'chaser for Lord Bicester. When his potential proved to be less actual than his connections had hoped, the show-ring proved to be a viable second string. He was produced in 1953, stood reserve to Mighty Atom at Windsor and was winning novice at Richmond. In 1954 he won again at Windsor and Richmond, and beat Mighty Atom in the championship at the Royal International, going on to win the Winston Churchill Cup.

One of the most outstanding patterns of a middleweight horse was the 1961 supreme champion at Dublin, Lady Helena Hilton-Green's (later Lady Daresbury) Last of Banogues. A brown 6-year-old by Dark Artist out of a mare by Tomahawk, his owner bought him from Ted Kelly of Camolin, Co Wexford, from whom she had already bought the brother, Banogue. He was a good racehorse and they made him favourite for the La Touche, with Pat Hogan riding; but he slipped up and broke his neck, besides knocking Pat out as well.

Last of Banogues had a very different life. He cost £150 as a 3-year-old and did three seasons hunting before he went to Dublin. He won to a tremendous ovation in Dublin and he was shown once more – at Peterborough the following year, where the judges were frightened of him – the rest of his life was all hunting, with Lady Daresbury first and then with her husband. He lived in retirement after his working life was over until he was 27, with another pensioner, Confidence, and an old kennel pony, and then he was put down before the winter. He was a 14 stone 7lb horse, and a real personality.

Perhaps the next outstanding middleweight, chronologically, was Master of the Blankney, Mr W. F. (Bill) Ransom's Spey Cast, a brown gelding by Nack, who was bred by the Hon Mrs Pretynan in 1960 and led champion at Lincoln, Rutland and Norfolk. He won the 4-year-old class at Newark, and championship at Leicester and Peterborough, and at both the Royal and the Hunter Show he wound up reserve champion to Harry Bonner on Robin Hood. In 1965 Lord Allenby, who ran the Richmond Royal, devised a heady and novel form of entertainment when he invited John Shedden to judge the classes and Colonel Neil Foster, joint-Master of the Grafton, to judge the championship. The only real danger to Spey Cast was Herb of Grace, a big soft chestnut, on the flash side, who had been his great rival since they were 3-year-olds. Most judges abhorred him, but John Shedden put him to win the middleweight class from Spey Cast, while in the championship, as we all knew he would, Neil Foster redressed the balance and put them the other way round!

It was the best entertainment of the year – except, perhaps, for the Royal Show, where the two met again. There Dick Francis broke his collar-bone when a horse slipped up with him, and Lord Daresbury, on his annual visit from Ireland to the show his father directed when he and his brother were boys, was press-ganged into taking over the

Plate 14 Mrs Bill Ransom on Spey Cast

judging, even though he was dressed as a spectator in a grey pin-striped lounge suit. The riders of the Canadian Cutting Horse display team conjured up a pair of leather chaps for him to put on over his trousers, Harry Bonner contributed his bowler hat and thus accoutred, His Lordship started to rejudge the whole class, very properly.

Now, Dick Francis had headed his line-up with Herb of Grace, ridden by Donald Owen. But Lord Daresbury had other ideas, and when Mr Owen found himself no longer at the head of the line, he rode the horse out of the ring – which did not go with a swing in the stands. The first in the line-up was, of course, Spey Cast, and he retained his supremacy over all-comers until, having in his 6-year-old year won the titles at the Royal, the Royal International and the Horse of the Year Show when ridden side-saddle by Rosalie Ransom, he was very properly retired to the hunting field.

Norman Crow's Top Notch, a splendid brown son of the premium stallion Top Walk, by Concerto out of May Queen by Gains-

50

borough, was bred near Thirsk in North Yorkshire by Guy Rob and foaled in 1962. Norman saw him at the Great Yorkshire Show, where he was fourth in his class as a 3-year-old. He needed time but he had great potential, and when he was 6 and 7 years old, in 1969 and 1970, he went to all the major shows and was unbeaten. Norman Crow reminisces about those days:

> I can just look out of the window and see him now, he's 24 years old and still has as much presence and character as he had then – he almost used to say to the judges: 'Here I am, look at me!' I hunted him three days a fortnight with the North Shropshire until he was 20, and he used to go to a county show a week in the summer. Richard Tomkinson, Master of the Cheshire, had his full brother and he was a Grade A show-jumper.

He was a memorable horse, and a rare pattern. Fair Gin, who followed him on, won a lot but was not in the same class.

Roy Trigg showed a good middleweight in Half Midnight, who was shown as a youngster by 'Gino' Henson, but he was sold to the

Plate 15 Mr Norman Crow on his Royal Show and Horse of the Year Show 1969 and 1970 Champion, Top Notch

United States quite early in the season.

In 1974 the Hunters' Improvement Society enlivened the scene considerably by announcing that all horses who had undergone the Hobday operation for afflictions of the wind – an operation invented in Germany and perfected by the President of the Royal Veterinary College, Professor Frederick Hobday – were to be debarred in future from the show-ring. The decision was made because Prince's Street, (whose owner, Vin Toulson, had never made any secret of the fact that the horse had been hobdayed) had a year earlier won all the major championships at leading shows although he was not, in effect, a sound horse. As most of those who complained were those whose horses had been beaten by Prince's Street, the furore was mainly attributable to one of the most ignoble of human emotions, that of jealousy.

However, the society, as custodians of the hunter, felt duty bound to take a stand, and the controversy waxed fast and furious as to whether a horse that had been cured of an unsoundness, by whatever means, could still in fairness be condemned as unsound and denied the entrée to a horse-show. Another aspect of the argument concerned the feasibility of testing horses suspected of having undergone the operation. Veterinary surgeons who have actually performed these operations, some in large numbers, declared that a successfully hobdayed horse is impossible to detect. A number of practitioners whose experience was more theoretical than practical were sure that accurate tests could be made by using an endoscope which, inserted into the nostril, lays bare all the secrets of the larynx on the principle of the periscope.

Those who felt most strongly formed themselves into a splinter group, representing exhibitors and owners, and made known their views at the AGM. They were heard with sympathetic courtesy and assured that the cessation of the hobday ban for working hunters might well be considered the following year. After the season started, rumours started to circulate that a certain import from Ireland who had been winning with a top professional had been hobdayed, and when he won the Champion of England Gold Cup at Peterborough, the putative Exhibitors' Association, still unconstituted but very vocal, objected to him. It was £25 down the drain. When the horse was bought, all the world was discussing the ban on hobdayed horses and the veterinary surgeon to the British teams, Peter Scott-Dunn, was instructed to examine him very carefully with regard to the state of his wind and his larynx. He passed the test with flying colours. Then the greatest British expert on the operation, Jeffrey Braine, confirmed that no operation had been performed on the larynx and that the horse was sound of his wind. Additionally, he had previously been vetted in Dublin by Professor Byrne, who corroborated what his colleagues had said.

The results occasioned the absolute rout of the splinter group, which then disintegrated.

The *Horse & Hound* Cup at the Royal in 1974 was won by Mrs Frank Furness' Seta Pike, home-bred in North Yorkshire by the premium stallion Kadir Cup, who also won the title at his own county show later the same month. He appeared again at the Horse of the Year Show, but failed to catch the judges' eye. A year later he regained both the *Horse & Hound* Cup and the Great Yorkshire title, but at the Horse of the Year Show he had the misfortune to run a foreign horse-shoe, floating loose in the ring, into his foot. Blood came pumping out of the sole and he was rushed off to the Royal Veterinary College with his distraught owners.

The next good middleweight to appear was Mrs Peter Warren's Middleton Lad, another son of Kadir Cup and Seta Pike's greatest rival. He won the Champion of England Gold Cup at Peterborough and beat Seta Pike in his class at the Royal International, but forfeited the latter prize when a routine dope test on the class winners proved positive to Butozolidin, which his owner admitted freely. She told me:

> He was going a bit 'feely' after Peterborough, having picked up some stones on the gravel track, so my vet told me to give him a course of powders for a week to settle down any inflammation. This course was finished two days before Wembley. As Middleton Lad also had a bit of a dry cough, I dosed him with a bottle of diaformin which we have had in the cupboard for years. I have since discovered that traces of Butozolidin can show in the urine for up to a fortnight after dosage has been discontinued. The first I knew of any trouble was a fortnight after the show, when I received a letter from Colonel Ansell enclosing a report from Newmarket Security.

Mrs Warren added that Middleton Lad had not been on bute all the summer and that David Barker, who had ridden him since the Royal Show, had no idea that the horse had had a course of powders.

Everyone felt very sorry for Mrs Warren, but agreed that for the good name of showing, justice had to be seen to be done. The horse was warned off for three months – effectively, to the end of the season – and Mrs Warren was prohibited from showing again for a year.

The next good middleweight to appear was Derek Cant's Dual Gold, a brown son of Le Dieu d'Or out of Ann Dual, who bred three winners. Dual Gold was bred by National Hunt steward Mr John Rose of Aslockton, Lincolnshire, and the horse was first spotted by Vincent and Daphne Toulson at the Doncaster Show and Sale in September, 1975. He was a promising 4-year-old and they tried to buy him then, bidding up to 4,500 guineas, only to find that his reserve was 5000. Later they rang to offer 5000 guineas only to learn that the horse had been sold into training. They asked for first refusal if he failed as a racehorse, to find that Lady Inchcape had bought him. Luckily, Vin had a show-jumper that she wanted, so at last Dual Gold arrived in their yard near Melton Mowbray.

He was sour and disinterested in his work, and not until Christmas did they dare to hope that their gamble might pay off. For months he failed to enjoy his work, and it was decided not to risk him in the hunting field but to give him a lot of galloping in company. He won his first championship at his first attempt, the Stoneleigh Spring Show, his second at the Hickstead Easter meeting and the third and most significant at Newark, a big agricultural show in Nottingham-shire where the form often holds good throughout the season. Under Captain Brian Fanshawe and Tony Martyn, the Toulsons won all three open weight classes – the lightweight with Magnum, by Kadir Cup, the middleweight with Dual Gold and the heavyweight with Mastermind.

Dual Gold was supreme again at Royal Windsor, beating Roy Trigg's former Dublin champion, Kit-Chin, and went on to take the Bath & West and South of England titles, after which Lady Zinnia Pollock made such a generous offer for him that he changed owners, though not stables. He was beaten on his first outing in new ownership, when Colonel Stephen Eve preferred the more hunter-like qualities of Langton Orchid, but after this minor setback he won the *Horse & Hound* Cup at the Royal, the Waterford Crystal Trophy at the Royal International and the Champion of England Gold Cup at Peterborough. Only at the Horse of the Year Show did his luck run out, and he dropped to an ignominious fourth place behind Seta Pike, Marion Stevenson's Cleveland-bred Overflow (another by Kadir Cup) and the comparatively unknown Orpheus.

Dual Gold's great strength lay in the ride he gave. One judge told me: 'I wondered what they all saw in him until I actually rode him. He is out of this world.' He was the only horse that Daphne Toulson could ride in comfort after fracturing her back. As a 6-year-old Robert Oliver bought him to show for Mrs Peter White from Sussex, and he went from strength to strength, being middleweight of the year at the Horse of the Year Show in 1977, 1978 and 1979. The following year, Robert's wife Gillian was unbeaten on him in working hunter classes and wound up winning the Wembley title. Every year he was well hunted and could jump any sort of fence from the Berkeley rhines to the Ledbury gates. Standing 17 hands and with 9in of bone, he was a horse and a half.

Vin Toulson is adept at finding champion hunters, and the grey Elite, by Manor Star, was one of his best finds. Bred in Wales by Mrs Unity Greenwood, he is HIS bred on both sides, being out of a mare by Accra, another good premium horse owned by Dyl Thomas of Neath, whose laugh is reminiscent of that of Harry Secombe. Also 17 hands and deep through the girth, standing on short legs, he came out in 1983 and consistently stood above a good Irishman, Mr and Mrs Sandison's liver chestnut Glenstawl, a winner since he arrived from Ireland to join Paul Rackham's string.

The most recent Toulson 'find' is Mr and Mrs Rose's Fireworks Night, who enjoyed his share of success and has now gone into training.

LIGHTWEIGHT

The true lightweight can carry from 12 to 13 stone and ideally should stand not much higher than 16.1hh, deep through and on a short leg, with good bone below the knee (not less than 8in, and preferably more), rather than those useless tall, long-legged, narrow animals that would hardly carry your boots. Some people seem to labour under the delusion that *height* carries weight. It does not: *bone* carries weight, and the horse that is deep and short-legged, standing 16 hands or thereabouts, can carry any weight. Lord Chaplin, who was Master of the Burton and the Blankney during the last half of the nineteenth century, and was also well known with the Belvoir, used to call out: 'Make way, make way – I'm 19 stone in my specs!' – and his weight-carriers were quality 15.3–16.1hh blood horses.

Although the lightweight horse that has to carry only 12st 7lb including saddle is far easier to breed than one up to more weight, and by the same token easier to find and to buy, a champion lightweight is seldom found. He must be really outstanding if he is to have the beating of a good middleweight or even a moderately good heavyweight, for it is the up-to-weight animals that command the highest prices and commercial value is, or should be, the deciding factor when it comes to a close decision. Again, however truly made a lightweight hunter may be, or however spectacular a mover and galloper, he seldom has the presence of the upper weight divisions' representatives. Moreover, the run-of-the-mill or average lightweight is inclined to be, however worthy, without that extra dimension that prints him indelibly on the memory.

There have, however, been exceptions, and the most memorable of them since the last war was Wavering Bee, a chestnut gelding by Wavetop, by the 1906 Derby winner Spearmint, out of Flying Bee by Honey Bee. Bred in Co Meath by Mr James Daly, and foaled in 1935, he was shown first at the Dublin Horse Show as a 4-year-old in 1939, where he swept all before him. He won the 4-year-old lightweight class, the open lightweight, the lightweight championship and finally the supreme hunter championship of the show, ridden and owned by Mr H. Davis Kenny. He was later bought by Mr W. H. Cooper, who kept him through the war and brought him out at Royal Windsor in 1946. For two seasons he was virtually unbeaten, and in addition to winning his class at Windsor (twice), Aldershot, City of Bath and Richmond Royal, he was champion at the White City and won the Champion of England Gold Cup at Peterborough. On each occasion he was competing against his immortal stable companion, Beau Geste.

Bee's great forte was his extravagant and spectacular movement in both his trot and his gallop, and although some were of the opinion that his action was unsuited to a hunter, the judges unanimously deemed him an exceptional ride. His way of going was probably inherited from his sire, for the Wavetops were spectacular goers. He was badly frightened by bombing during the war, but Miss Matkin, who showed him so well, regained his confidence.

Then came the brown Holyport, who lacked the courage of his predecessor but stood supreme for two seasons. By Steel Point, registered in the GSB as Jimmy Steel, he was bred in Ireland in 1942 out of Terpsichore and was sold by Mr Horace Smith to Eric Wilson and produced by Count Robert Orssich in 1948 to win the novice,

Plate 16 Miss Matkin on Mr W. H. Cooper's Wavering Bee, winner of the lightweight class at Dublin in 1939, and in England after the war

lightweight and ladies' classes at Richmond, and at most of the major subsequent shows. In October he was bought by Mrs Selwyn Butcher, who had started showing a favourite hunter to please her groom, who taught her to ride side-saddle.

When Mrs Butcher's husband could no longer bear to see her in the back row he decided to give her a show horse. When she first rode him she was quite unable to hold him in the gallop, but luckily he could always find an extra leg to get him around the corners. She learned afterwards that the Count remarked to her husband: 'Well, at least she is not frightened to let him go!' Little did he know! But Holyport won the Richmond lightweight class three times off the reel, and his name is on every lightweight cup of note. He also hunted weekly with the New Forest Buckhounds.

Two outstanding lightweights both made their initial bow at

Dublin in 1951 — Patricia Cope's Mighty Grand and Ronnie Marmont's Cufflink. The former, by Steadlis, by Felstead out of Cora, a hunter mare, who won point-to-points in the West of Ireland, was bred by Mrs Neasham, for whom he won each year from his foalhood. But at Dublin Mrs Tollit rode him for Nat Galway-Greer. Then 6, he won the open lightweight, ladies' lightweight and both championships, and was bought by Miss Cope (later Mrs Shaw). In 1955, his best season, he swept the board at Harringay, winning lightweight and champion Hunter of the Year titles and was Riding Horse of the Year over 15.2hh.

Cufflink, by Bachelor's Convert, out of a mare by Ben Alder, was bred by Bartholomew Cuff, shown in Dublin by Eamonn Rohan, the well-known farmer-dealer from Middleton, Co Cork, whose son Jerry is carrying on the good work. He won the lightweight 4-year-old class and was reserve to Mighty Grand for the cup after a most impressive gallop. He came to England in the autumn and was very sharp on arrival, refusing to be mounted from the ground. In his first English season he was champion at Rutland, in 1953 he was winning lightweight and under side-saddle at White City and won at Richmond and Aldershot. In 1954 his successes included two classes at Windsor, the Hunter Show and International, and won the Hunter title at Harringay. In 1955 he continued virtually to 'farm' the ladies' classes and won at Newark, the Hunter Show, the Great Yorkshire and Peterborough, Windsor, Richmond, the Royal and the White City. In 1956 he retired to the hunting field, the dip in his back having become very pronounced.

Mrs Jean Wood's incomparable Prince's Grace, whom I have already dealt with in the chapter on brood mares, was the outstanding lightweight and ladies' hunter of the late Fifties and early Sixties. She was followed by the Hon Mrs Stella Cardiff's Palladium, by Top Walk, shown by Jack Gittins, whose great gallop enabled him to win many championships — at Windsor the Queen once remarked what a great galloper he was. In 1962, as a novice 5-year-old, he won at Windsor, Richmond, the Three Counties, the Royal and the Horse of the Year Show, where he was reserve champion. In 1963 he won at Oxford and Windsor, Richmond, the Royal Highland, Lincoln, the Hunter Show and the Royal. At Peterborough he won the Gold Cup and at the Royal International he took the lightweight and ladies' classes. The next year he successfully defended the Gold Cup at Peterborough. He ended his career doing what he loved best —

Plate 17 Michael Hickey on Mrs Roy Latta's 5-year-old Frozen Slave, the 1968 Dublin Supreme and Lightweight Champion by Arctic Slave (Fiona Forbes)

carrying Major Bob Hoare, Master of the South Notts, in the hunting field before being pensioned off at Armscote to a cosseted retirement with his old friends.

Next of the greats was Monbra, bred at Bracknell by Mrs Michael Smallwood, by Hop Bridge, out of Mona XI, by Forerunner. He was sold as a young horse to Miss Judy Frank in the Duke of Beaufort's country and then to Mrs John Moss — better known as Rosemary Cooke. His first two seasons in the ring, 1964–5, were not conspicuously successful, but in 1966 he could do no wrong and his triumphal progress started at the Bath & West and encompassed Richmond Royal, the Royal, the Royal Internationl and the Horse of the Year Show, where he took the Hunter title. He had by now acquired Miss Betsy Profumo as a joint owner. At the start of his career he was undistinguished, and was somewhat of a whippers-in type horse, but he grew into presence and quality.

Perhaps the most recent outstanding lightweight was Brewster, who won at every age for Robert Oliver, both in-hand and under both saddles, culminating as lightweight of the year at Wembley. But unequivocally the most successful of all was Andy and Jane Crofts' bay Periglen, by Graham Heal's good North Devon premium stallion, The Ditton, out of Lovely Valley, by Spiritus. Periglen, sold for the proverbial song as a 15 hands 3in 3-year-old at the HIS Show and sale at Taunton racecourse in 1980, was to continue growing until he was 6, adding a hand to his stature. He won as a 3-year-old at Newbury and won the championship there six years later. He was defeated only twice in 1986, and won the Peterborough Gold Cup in three consecutive years, the only horse ever to achieve this feat. Having won nearly £8,000 during his three years in the ring, he now goes into training.

THE WORKING HUNTER

The Working Hunter (initial capitals intended) was never heard of in the British Isles until a few years after the end of World War II, when the idea was imported from the USA. The object was to give an outlet in the show-ring for the horse who was not the most glorious mover nor the best-looking horse imaginable standing still, but to the good sort of animal who is, above all, a performer, able to give a good account of himself over a fair course of predominantly natural fences.

They did not catch on with judges or with the largest proportion of exhibitors for a long time. The horse world is always wary of innovation, its older members especially so, and there were dark mutterings about the classes being merely competitions for the best-looking show-jumpers, with added dark prophesies that in a few years' time everything in the ring that was broken to saddle would have to jump, 'Just as they do in America!'

This was forty years ago, and none of these dire happenings have come to pass (in fact, horses have to jump in America, I have been told by knowledgeable Americans, only because they have hardly any conformation judges left there, which is thankfully not the state yet over here). The Working Hunter class is here to stay, and has given a

great deal of fun to young people with the not-quite top-class horse –
and to those not so young in years as in heart who possess one of
those horses which Snaffles depicted in his classic print, entitled
''Andsome is as 'andsome does'.

Some Working Hunters, indeed, have gone on to great heights.
Rita Burch, a farmer's daughter from Lincolnshire, won the Working
Hunter of the Year title at Wembley on a grand sort of workmanlike
type of middleweight animal by the premium hunter stallion,
Evening Trial, who stood in Yorkshire. The horse was called
Goodwill. He was bought by the Queen as a potential three-day
event horse for Princess Anne and she rode him in the 1976 Olympic
Games in Montreal. Another well-known winning Working Hunter
who soared to dizzy heights of international success was Mary
Gordon-Watson's Cornishman, who won the European Individual
Championship at Haras du Pin (Normandy) in 1969, the World
Championship over the same course in Co Kildare in 1970 and an
Olympic team gold medal in Munich in 1972. Another was Judy
Bradwell's Castlewellan, who became a more than useful three-day
event horse. In fact, the Working Hunter classes make a good nursery
for either category of international horse, and their ranks are now
scrutinised regularly for those seeking likely recruits, both in England
and in Dublin, where there are now three categories of what they call
Performance Champions which occupy the morning of the penulti-
mate, Aga Khan Trophy day.

The thing that took the longest time to fall into place was the
actual course over which the Working Hunters had to disport
themselves before their ride and conformation were assessed. In the
early days they were comprised very largely of staring, shiny red and
white poles, identical to those used for novice jumping competitions.
At last the course builders, nurtured as they were on show-jumping
rather than hunters, got the message about rustic poles, tanalised or
creosoted gates and stiles, straw bales – all the natural materials.
Some adventuring spirits conceived brilliant touches like leaving a
tractor running beside or between fences. The Royal stages an annual
championship over an excellent course in the main ring, with
substantial, natural-looking fences. Sponsored by Strutt & Parker, it
is a qualifier both for the championship at the Hunter Show and at
the Horse of the Year Show.

The working classes are definitely here to stay and are popular
with many of the more amateur exhibitors, who regard them as a

Plate 18 Lavinia, Duchess of Norfolk's Penny Royal, Show Hunter of the Year and later Working Hunter of the Year

useful schooling ground, as indeed they are.

Lavinia, Duchess of Norfolk, owned a splendid Working Hunter, Penny Royal, who was also Show Hunter of the Year at Wembley in 1953 as well, and Working Hunter of the Year two years later, when he was unbeaten in these classes. A brown gelding, 16.3hh, foaled in 1948 and bred in Co Cork by Maurice Hennessy, he was by Obligato out of a mare by Mount Edgar. Mr Harry Frank bought him as a 2-year-old and sold him that autumn to the late Colonel C.H.S. Townsend. After winning the 4-year-old class at the Three Counties he was bought by the Duchess. The next year he won at the White City and took the Harringay title. In 1955, besides winning the Harringay Working Hunter title and scoring at Badminton, Windsor and Richmond, he went hunting as usual, and another of his activities, which he thoroughly enjoyed, was to carry the starter at Ascot.

THE SMALL HUNTER

The late Mr Justice Wylie, for over a quarter of a century the benevolent dictator of the Royal Dublin Society's Horse Show, was a very wise man. For many years he declined firmly to include classes for small hunters in the programme. When I asked him why, he replied: 'Because there are enough small horses being bred by mistake, without encouraging them to be bred on purpose!'

He was so right, of course, and the 15 hands 2in horse is generally either a young person's hunter, after they have graduated from ponies, or a misfit, although there are those who are lightweights and simply like small horses, which many do not, even though small horses are more economical to keep than those exceeding 16 hands. At any rate, as a show category they are here to stay, but there have been few memorable ones and there are not great crowds waiting to see them shown.

One who was memorable, however, was Burrough Hills, who came out of Leicestershire, although he was actually bred in Northamptonshire, by Major R. Bourne of Towcester, in 1947, by Grey Metal out of Norah's Star. He was bought by that well-known judge, Mrs George Gibson, wife of the Oakham veterinary surgeon, for her two sons, but he was somewhat too high couraged for them when young. His first big win came at the Leicestershire Show, where he won his class and was reserve champion, and he went on to win at the Hunter Show, Bath, the Great Yorkshire and the Royal Lancashire, as well as becoming champion hunter at Thame. In 1955 he was unbeaten in twenty-five outings, his victories including Royal Windsor, Richmond Royal, a class of thirty at the Royal International and the Riding Horse of the Year title at Harringay. He was supreme again in 1956, when his most notable victories were Windsor, Richmond, the White City, the Royal and the Hunter Show. At the Royal Lancashire he sustained his only defeat in two seasons, apart from the Small Hunter title at Harringay in 1955, where the class conditions entailed the negotiation of a jumping course as well as the customary showing procedure.

Burrough Hills was bought by Ronnie Marmont in 1954 and he was usually ridden by Miss Ailsa Smith-Maxwell, daughter of the late distinguished hunting correspondent of *The Field*, now Mrs Nigel Pease, herself a respected judge. In those days small hunters were often known as Young People's or Juvenile Hunters, but they

Plate 19 Mrs Nigel Pease on R. Marmant's protégé small hunter, Burrough Hills

soon had to be thrown open as so many people over 21 years of age enjoyed riding them.

Mrs Rosemary Cooke, who started her adult showing life with cobs at the end of World War II, later switched to small hunters with equal success. The first of them was Tomboy, a charming bay gelding who went back to the famous polo pony stallion, Mallinin, by Malice. Then came Some Gardener, bought by Mrs Cooke and her husband, John Moss, at the Ascot sales and out of that good 'chasing mare, Miss Maru, dam of Red Maru. The last was Lord Sorceror, by the premium stallion More Magic. His owner became very ill after acquiring him and he was sold on to Major Helme, Master of the South Herefordshire, and gave Robert Oliver his first successes for three years at the start of his career, winning at many of the leading shows, including the Horse of the Year.

Mrs Cooke started her showing career as Miss Rosemary Schwader, riding show ponies at Olympia for the late Horace Smith, who had stables in Cadogan Mews, off Sloane Street, which was very handy for Hyde Park and the urban delights of Rotten Row; he also had more rural stables at Holyport, near Maidenhead, which was handy for Windsor Castle. Not only did he and his daughter, Miss Sybil Smith, teach the Queen and Princess Margaret to ride when they were children, they also instructed all the young members of the Royal Family – the Kents, the Gloucesters and the Harewoods, plus the Westmorlands and many, many more. I ghosted Horace's book in my youth, entitled *A Horseman Through Six Reigns*, which he was, starting with Queen Victoria and ending with our present Queen. He was a delightful and courtly old gentleman, held in high esteem by all, and his daughter is a splendid, most kindly person.

Another big winner was Pelicamp, a marvellous son of The Pelican who was bred in Yorkshire by the Halls, where he won three times on the flat before the daughters of the family started showing him. Then he was sold into Cornwall and became the property of Miss Judith Lawrey, an indefatigable traveller from her father Melville's farm near Land's End to shows as far distant as Newark and Lincoln. Pelicamp was a great winner in the Sixties when these classes really needed winning, and he won at the highest level with championships at all the major shows and the Small Hunter title at the Horse of the Year Show.

In 1966 I advertised in *Horse & Hound* for a sensible horse to ride with my children, the telephone rang and there was Judy, saying: 'Would you like me to give you Pelicamp? We are not going to show him any more, and we want a good home for him.' I could hardly believe my ears, but I went down to lunch and found that 'Peli' was the best ride I had ever sat on, and so home he came. Sadly, he had been 'got at' at Newark Show. Judy visited him in the early morning, noticed a disreputable character coming from that direction in a hurry, and found Pelicamp down in his box. He remained down for three days, during which time the two-day show took place around him and everyone went home. The vet said that he had definitely been nobbled, and although he had always enjoyed going off to a show, he now showed a marked reluctance to enter the box, so he was retired.

We had him for five years and he was greatly loved, so it was a great sadness when I was at the Royal International to be told on the telephone by my husband that Peli had been found by the field gate with a compound fracture of a hind leg, just below the hock, and had been shot and taken to the kennels. He was so gentle that if one sat down beside him in his box he would put his head in one's lap.

Mrs Vivian Bishop had an outstanding small hunter mare by Vulgan called Debutante IV, which she bought at Dublin where she won as a yearling, from Diana Edge, sister to Mrs William Hanson. Mrs Bishop hunted her with her husband's Golden Valley hounds in Herefordshire until she was 11, then Vivian rode her for two more seasons after a bad fall, and finally she was put in foal for the first time and proceeded to have 6 progeny – 4 sons and 2 daughters. Her daughter by Grasi's Son, who won the Mecca Dante, is still hunting and all her children hunted, hunter trialled and evented.

HUNTER · FOUNDATION STOCK

THE CLEVELAND BAY

Yorkshire has long been famed as a horse-breeding county, producing big, upstanding stock, and no breed has brought more honour to its native heath than the Cleveland Bay. In medieval days a race of clean-legged horses, traditionally bay in colour, was used for agricultural and pillion purposes, and they were bred in great numbers in the Cleveland district. The 'chapmen', or travelling salesmen, especially favoured them for carrying their packs of goods to towns and villages all over England, so that the breed became known as 'chapman' horses, and attracted attention for their beauty and action. Before the days of coaches, with the roads axle-deep in ruts, travelling for vehicles was so slow that not only did men journey on horseback, they also carried corn, coal, wool and farm produce packed on the backs of horses, which had to be strong, sure-footed and fast walkers.

The earliest coaches arrived in the reign of Queen Elizabeth I, and the Cleveland Bay was well suited to the task of drawing these big, heavy vehicles. Early in the nineteenth century John Macadam was responsible for improving the road surfaces so that the coaches were able to travel at 10 miles an hour, and breeders turned to blood to increase pace. The Cleveland horse had been kept religiously free of cart blood, and as the speed of travel increased, so did the Cleveland Bay undergo heavier and heavier infusions of Thoroughbred blood – in fact, every horse in the Stud Book can be traced back to eighteenth-century racing sires. After coaching days came the railways, and the family coach was replaced by the carriage and pair, so once again Cleveland mares were mated to big Thoroughbreds. The progeny, who had perhaps 25 per cent of *new* Thoroughbred blood in their veins, came to be known as the Yorkshire Bay Coach Horses or New Cleveland Bays, to distinguish them from the Old

Cleveland Bay, a distinctly separate and ancient breed; and they commanded a ready market all over the world.

At the end of the last century it was found that the tendency was towards too much blood, and recourse was had to the old Cleveland Bay strains. In 1886 the Yorkshire Coach Horse Society was formed, and all pure CB stallions were admitted to its stud book. The Cleveland farmers still stuck to their old strains, but during the 1880s a great market arose in the USA, and as farming was none too profitable or remunerative at this time, hundreds upon hundreds of the breed left the Cleveland area forever.

The first stud books of foundation stock were published in 1884 and 1885. No drop of carting blood, no matter how far back, was admitted, and although a strain of Thoroughbred blood could be found a long way back in the male line, the type was fixed in the eighteenth century and has remained true and been kept clear of alien infusions ever since.

Fantastic records are claimed for the Cleveland Bay, one of which trotted 16 miles in an hour, carrying 16 stone, while another carried 700lb for 60 miles in 24 hours four times a week, while many a Cleveland has travelled from Hyde Park Corner to York in three days. The founders of the Cleveland Bay Society laid down that the horse should stand about 16 hands, and have a shortish back, with muscular loins, deep, sloping, muscular shoulders, level and powerful quarters and 9–10½in of bone below the knee. The days when every farmer in Yorkshire kept them are gone, but many, realising the value of their heritage, not only as work-horses but also for grading up the native breeds and as a foundation stock for hunter breeding, have hung on to their animals. The USA has its own Cleveland Bay Society, and many of the best weight-carrying hunters in the world have been bred by Thoroughbred stallions out of Cleveland Bay mares, or by Thoroughbred stallions out of half-bred mares whose sire was a CB.

Mr George Duell of Staithes is a very keen supporter of the breed, which receives an annual grant not only from the Racecourse Betting Control Board but from the Ministry of Agriculture and the British Horse Society. His father before him showed many good horses, and he commenced showing foals by TB stallions out of CB mares. In 1955 he won every CB championship, either with his home-bred Mulgrave Contralto or his 3-year-old stallion Mulgrave. Contralto was by Farnley Exchange out of Mulgrave Star, who won at the

Royal and the Great Yorkshire, and dam of Mulgrave by Lord Halifax. Both won from foalhood, and Mulgrave Contralto was also champion at Harrogate and the Royal.

Mr W. Keenleyside of Scorton also had a famous mother and son when he was president of the CBHS. The mare, Lady Fairfax, 16.2hh, was bred in 1940 by the CBH syndicate, and when bought she was so poor that it was conceded that he should withhold payment for three months in the event of her dying. However, she bred a foal as a 3-year-old and went on to become female champion at the Royal twice. Her son Lord Fairfax, 17 hands by Aerobatic, won the Sir Alfred Pease Memorial Urn as a foal and was thrice champion at the Royal and the Great Yorkshire. He and his dam lived out all the year round and only received hay when there was snow on the ground.

Miss Mary Furness, a former Master of the Hurworth, bred many good CB × TB cross-breds which she and her brother hunted, and one of them, a mare called North Flight, was in the British Olympic show-jumping team with William Barker in Tokyo in 1964.

The Cleveland has come into its own yet again with the advent of Combined Driving competitions, and the Duke of Edinburgh regularly drives a team of Cleveland Bays, some crossed with Oldenburgers. When not competing, these horses are used in coaches on the streets of London doing ceremonial duties.

The most outstanding Cleveland Bay of recent years has been the stallion Mulgrave Supreme. To prevent his going for export to the United States, the Crown Equerry, Colonel Sir John Miller, mentioned him to the Queen and she purchased him in order that he might remain in this country and be available to breeders. He stood at stud near York with Max Abram and his team of HIS premium stallions, and covered a great many hunter mares of the type who required additional bone and substance in their progeny. A dark bay, 17hh and foaled in 1961, he was by Cholderton Minstrel out of Mulgrave Rose. In 1962 he went to Windsor, was broken in 1964 and proved himself a good, willing jumper, a straight and active mover with a particularly good temperament, quiet in single and double harness. He was first at stud in Oxfordshire, then went back into regular work at Windsor and remained quiet in every way. He then stood in Leicestershire until 1970, when he was moved back to Yorkshire. His stud fee was 20 guineas. In 1962, 1965 and 1970 he won the King George V Cup at Redcar. On the only other occasion

Plate 20 HM The Queen's Cleveland Bay stallion, Mulgrave Supreme

on which he was shown, he was champion at the Great Yorkshire
Show in 1963.

Cholderton Minstrel, the sire of Mulgrave Supreme, was bred at
Captain L. Edmunds' stud at Cholderton, near Salisbury, Wiltshire.
The stud has been in existence for more than seventy years. Minstrel
was never shown, but was considered to be one of the best stallions
bred at this stud since the last war. As for Mulgrave Rose, the dam of
Mulgrave Supreme, she was generally acknowledged to be the best
Cleveland Bay mare bred since the war. She was the winner of
innumerable prizes, including the Watson Challenge Cup at the
Stockton Show in 1957, the championship at the Great Yorkshire
Show in 1959, 1960, 1961, 1964 and 1965. From 1959 to 1965 she
was likewise champion at the Royal Show.

Mulgrave Rose, her dam Mulgrave Contralto and her grandam
Mulgrave Star, were all great winners in the show-ring and great
brood mares. Mulgrave Rose has two sons in the United States, her
only surviving daughter bred well and her great-grand-daughter
Gilishaw Katrina was regarded as the outstanding filly of her
generation.

Within his own breed, Mulgrave Supreme was the sire of, among others, Forest Superman, foaled in 1964, winner at the Royal, champion at the Great Yorkshire and winner of the King George V Cup at Redcar in 1966, 1968 and 1969. He also sired Forest Fable in 1965, another big winner; Knaresborough Warlock, who won the Royal in 1970 and was Breed Champion at the Great Yorkshire, and Principal Boy, who, having won the Royal and the Great Yorkshire, was exported to Japan.

The most renowned Cleveland cross-bred event horse is Count Colunna's John of Gaunt, who won the Burghley Horse Trials in 1980 with Richard Walker. His dam was a Thoroughbred mare.

THE IRISH DRAUGHT

Although the story of the Irish Draught horse since World War II has been devastatingly close to the old saw about locking the stable door after the horse has gone, with the luck of the Irish they have succeeded pretty well in saving – or perhaps resuscitating is a better word – the age-old breed, which has been responsible for all the wonderful hunters for which Ireland has been famed for at least the last four hundred years. And although those who remember the old breed of Draught horse between the wars maintain that the modern one is a totally different animal, and nothing like as good as its predecessor, it was still pretty clever to salvage anything at all, considering that most of the mares were sent to abattoirs in Belgium and Holland after the war to be eaten by those who regard horses as comestibles, which are mercifully not to the taste of the denizens of the British Isles.

Although the modern Irish Draught horse is said to be an Irish fairy tale, it is unlikely that too many Irish farmers would care to throw a saddle on it after driving it in the plough all the week and take it hunting on Sundays as their forefathers used to do, because they really are more reminiscent of the plough than the saddle. Their only real drawbacks are the immense height of some of them (pointing to perhaps a Clydesdale background not too far removed) and their strong tendency to be back of their knees, which is a very serious fault because they almost invariably break down in the end with work. But they are still wide, deep and useful, with excellent bone, and they have clean legs without much feather.

To assist in the preservation and promotion of the breed, and to improve the standard through careful selection of breeding stock, is

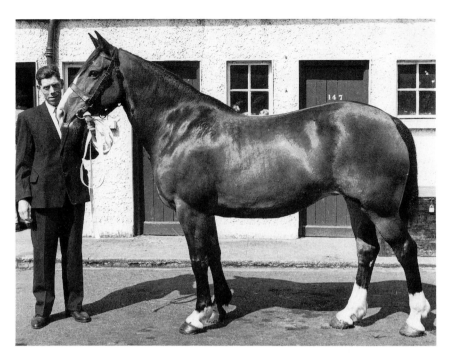

Plate 21 Irish Draught mare Island Rambler at Dublin to see her son, Never Forget, by Blue Cliff, stand Supreme Champion in 1966 (G. A. Duncan)

the chief aim of the Irish Draught Horse Society, which is based in Enniskeane, Co Cork. It has an official list or panel of approved judges and has drawn up a standard. Formed in 1976, there are now thirteen county branches and Northern Ireland and Great Britain have branches which are co-ordinated through a central council.

One of the nicest Irish Draught mares I ever saw was a little brown cobby animal with a great deal of quality called Island Rambler. She was by Merrion, and I saw her at the Royal Dublin Society Horse Show in 1967, where her son Never Forget, a big brown 4-year-old by the Preciptic horse Blue Cliff, who stood with Timothy Carey at the Tullaghansleek Stud, Castletowngeoghegan, Co Waterford, had just won the supreme hunter championship and the heavyweight cup, ridden by the legendary Jack Gittins for the likewise legendary Nat Galway-Greer.

Although one or two people tried to buy Never Forget to bring to England, he was sold to Italy to be hunted by an Italian heavyweight with the Roman Foxhounds, who are kennelled on the Appian Way and fed, so it is said, on pasta. It seemed a hard fate for a lovely horse.

Island Rambler's connections had applied, without success, to have her registered as an Irish Draught mare, but she was spurned because she was under 15.2 hands high. However, when her son, some 17 hands, achieved such distinction, she received an invitation to join this exclusive club!

A few years afterwards at the National Hunter Show at Shrewsbury I saw a very nice bay mare winning the small hunter brood mare class for Mrs G. Block of Meadle, near Aylesbury. I looked up her breeding in the catalogue and discovered to my delight that she was by Blue Cliff out of Island Rambler by Merrion, and thus a small, year-younger full sister to the Dublin champion. She had a lovely home on a farm and I subsequently learned that she was a brilliant hunter before she became a brood mare, and went back to the hunting field when she decided to take a year off her maternal duties, on which she was not over-enthusiastic as a steady diet. Nevertheless, she bred six live foals and one still-born, her sons include an eventer

Plate 22 Jack Gittins on Mr Nat Galway-Greer's Never Forget, by Blue Cliff out of Island Rambler, Supreme Champion at Dublin in 1966 (G. A. Duncan)

called Barney Dillon and her last foal, born in 1986 when she was 24, is a daughter to follow her on. Her owner bought her at the Thame Show because she was barren and the previous owner had to part with her.

So Island Rambler, who bred a champion heavyweight one year and a champion small hunter brood mare the next, brought nothing but credit to the Irish Draught horse. There are now four Irish Draught stallions who have been inspected by the panel of the Hunters' Improvement Society and approved as sires to cover owners' mares, with three Welsh cobs and one Cleveland Bay, Mr D. W. Keenleyside's Forest Superman, a son of the Queen's Mulgrave Supreme.

The Irish Draught stallions are the Warwickshire College of Agriculture's Clonfert, M. E. Maryan's Enniskean Pride, G. McMaster's Colman and A. L. Smith-Maxwell's Skippy. This is a very wise move indeed to get some bone and substance back into the British-bred mares who may lack these qualities, an essential part of their stock-in-trade – especially when it has been proven that the sort of courage required by hunters and event horses is not normally the prerogative of the continental breeds, however much their protagonists may declaim their virtues.

THE · SHOW · HACK

When I last compiled a book about champion horses and ponies, in 1956, the show hack was still in its heyday. Unhappily, it has since gone into what can only be described as a decline. There are, of course, still hacks about, and some of them – particularly the 'large' variety (that is, those from 15 to 15.3hh) – are still, *nearly* as good as they were before. Those not exceeding 15hh, however, the small hacks, have ceased to be little horses and become either overgrown ponies or Araby monstrosities with hooky hind legs, elevated tail carriage and straight shoulders.

Everyone of the experts agrees, to a greater or a lesser degree, that 'the type has been lost', but no one seems to know quite why. For the essence of the show hack are his beauty, grace and elegance, both standing still and even more in motion – he glides around the ring, pointing his toes and putting them out in long, low strides – and his manners. He is judged for conformation in the same way as is a hunter, or any other riding horse; but whereas a well-made hunter can get away with a certain plainness – which may well make him appear all the more a workman – such is not the case with a hack. He must be a thing of beauty and elegance with presence, that hard-to-define superiority and poise that compels and holds the attention of the spectator when the horse enters the ring, which is equally important, while manners are a sine qua non.

No one has yet been able to tell us in so many words exactly what a hack should be, nor yet his purpose in life. In the old days there was the park hack, whose use in life is self-explanatory, and the covert hack, on which his owner would ride from home to the meet, before the days of motor horse-boxes, there to change over to his hunter, which had been ridden on by a groom. Today, the show hack and the park hack are probably nearly similar in that both, presumably, are pleasant to ride and also to look upon. Yet even this description comes nowhere near to defining the highly controversial 'hack type', which phrase is bandied about by critics of the hack classes, who aver that such-and-such either has, or more frequently has not, this desirable but elusive quality which they are so singularly unable to define; for his supporters would have us believe that the Arab horse is the most pleasant ride of any horse, yet no Arab ever wins any class but those specifically confined exclusively to Arabs.

If one may be permitted to attempt to deduce a type from the great hacks who have won in the past, and the handful of outstanding animals who were winning forty years ago, and the odd two or three who are winning today, he/she is a lovely quality horse with adequate substance, either Thoroughbred or nearly so, as nearly perfect in conformation as possible and, without being in any sense a weed, yet considerably finer-drawn than the hunter, for he is not called upon to spend long days jumping into nor out of heavy going – even in the unlikely event of his having to leave the ground at all. He has an abundance of presence, so that as soon as he enters the ring he becomes the cynosure of all eyes, yet less fire than the hunter, for outstanding courage is by no means essential, if even desirable, in the horse on which one disports oneself in the park before breakfast,

Plate 23 June, unbeaten 1946 Champion Hack and dam of many champion hacks and a HIS brood mare (W. W. Rouch & Co)

perhaps without even so much as a cup of tea to dispel the cobwebs. His action must be more showy than that of the hunter – in the show-ring an exaggerated pointing of the toe at the trot, although it can be the acme of discomfort to the rider, will speed a novice hack along the road to fame.

As for the proverbial 'hack canter' which is notable for its smoothness, its effortless collection and its rhythmic cadence, it has all the comforts of the highest class armchair with added motion. This pace perhaps provides the greatest test of the quality show hack as far as movement and paces are concerned, for while the mediocre animal scratches along with stilted strides, the champion moves fluidly and effortlessly forward, his hocks well under him, reaching for the ground with his perfect sloping shoulders and long, low strides.

The hack is not required to gallop, and a gentle tittup is the only extended pace that is required of him, although some exhibitors conclude their individual show with a rousing gallop, followed by a halt and unhurried rein-back, to prove that their charges can even indulge in the excitement of a gallop without having either a heart attack or hysterics – but these are the experts.

To compensate for not being required to gallop, the hack is not allowed to get away with just a walk, trot and canter but has to demonstrate his ability to answer the leg, rein back, change rein, etc, in what is termed the individual show. These callisthenics are performed individually in line-up order, and the extent and nature of the show is determined by the skill and ambition of the rider. The expert will usually give a simple show which is 100 per cent perfect in every detail. If the horse makes a mistake he capitalises on it, pretending that the mistake was, in fact, his intention. He is always nonchalant and as impassive as a poker player, displaying enviable sang froid.

Hacks are judged 50 per cent on conformation, presence and action and 50 per cent on ride, manners and training. There are two categories, large and small, except at the leading shows like the Royal, the Royal Windsor, Royal International and Horse of the Year Show, where there is also a class for ladies' hacks to be ridden side-saddle, which is always well worth seeing. There used also to be a pairs class at a few select shows, but the difficulty in matching horses and the shortage of men's overalls and top hats caused it to be dropped.

Plate 24 Liberty Light, Champion Hack for three post-war seasons (W. W. Rouch & Co)

The first outstanding hack to be shown after World War II was Liberty Light, who was produced and ridden from Winkfield Row, near Windsor, by Count Robert Orssich, an Austro-Hungarian. Registered in the General Stud Book as Pearl Harbour, he was a brown gelding, foaled in 1940, by Fairford out of Cyl-Molluscia, who was one of twins. An indifferent racehorse, he won twice on the flat and then once or twice over hurdles, after which he was 'discovered', the rogue horse in the trainer's yard, by Colonel Dan Corry of the Irish Army show-jumping team, who spotted that he was a champion hack in the making. He was bought by Mrs Barbara Harcourt-Wood, who sent him to Count Orssich to produce, and then he made his first appearance at Windsor in 1949 to win the championship. He proceeded to rule the roost for three seasons for various owners, including Mrs Selwyn Butcher, being hailed as the best hack to have been seen since the Thirties with his airy, buoyant movement and abundant liberty. He won the Royal Windsor, Richmond Royal and Royal International championships three times in succession, plus the Winston Churchill Cup and the Hack of the Year title. When, in 1951, he won the Richmond accolade for the last time, he was ridden by Mr Horace Smith, the Royal Family's riding master, who was then 74 years of age.

Next, in 1952, came Honeysuckle, the eldest daughter of June, who won at the White City with Count Orssich in 1946 for Mrs Noel Edwards, his wife at that time, as recounted on p27. Honeysuckle, by Henry Wynmalen's Basa Shagya, was bred and owned by Miss Marguerite de Beaumont, and after winning in-hand classes in her youth, became *the* hack of the 1952 season, winning all the big prizes. Her appearance was arresting and her movement spectacular – her greatest attribute, in fact, but she had too many of the Arab traits for the purist and at the end of her only season as a ridden hack she was allowed to retire to found another dynasty.

The next outstanding hack was Mrs Christopher Mackintosh's Blithe Spirit, one of the best I have ever seen. He and his owner were

Plate 25 Mrs Christopher Mackintosh and Blithe Spirit, who typified the grace and quality of the hack (W. W. Rouch & Co)

a supremely elegant combination, and quite strikingly successful, as they well deserved to be. A brown son of The Grey Abbot out of a mare by Hot Haste, Archie Thomlinson of Grewelthorpe, near Ripon, sold him to the triple Badminton winner, Sheila Willcox, in 1953. Mrs Mackintosh fell in love with him when she saw him at Royal Windsor, asked for first refusal there and bought him after he won the championship at the International. He was only once defeated in ladies' classes thereafter and he won three successive championships at Windsor. In 1956 he was the undisputed champion of the year, among his successes being Richmond and the International as well as Windsor and Harringay.

Honeysuckle proved to be a fertile mare at stud, and she kept an *embarras de richesse* of young hacks flowing towards the show-ring, somewhat to the consternation of Count Orssich, who was not enamoured of them. First there was Ladybird, who had a most unengaging temperament. When the count had a disagreement with Miss de Beaumont he was able to sigh with relief and say, 'Thank heaven I shall not have to have any more of that terrible family.' So Harry Tatlow had the dubious pleasure and privilege of battling with Juniper, whose temperament was, if anything, worse than Ladybird's, although he was at least somewhat more comely. To the best of my recollection, he became Show Hack of the Year at the Horse of the Year Show (which moved to Wembley in 1959). At all events, when he first appeared as a novice at Windsor, Colonel John Smith-Maxwell, hunting correspondent to *The Field*, was moved to write in the *Horseman's Year* (edited by Colonel Ted Lyon): 'Dior [produced by Count Orssich for Hugh Haldin and ridden by Ann Davy] has a little to learn, Juniper appears to have quite a little to forget!'

However, when she was mated to the polo pony stallion Clieveden Boy, the temperament improved greatly. Shalbourne Last Waltz was ridden by David Tatlow on two occasions to be Small Hack of the Year at Wembley in 1970 and 1971, while Shalbourne Honeymoon was the winner of the HIS Champion Challenge Cup for the best brood mare in the show at the National Hunter Show at Shrewsbury in 1974 – not bad going for a little one!

I am getting ahead of myself with all these obstetrical details. After a few lean years, the next outstanding hack to appear was Miss Alicia Stubbings's Desert Storm, by the French Anglo-Arab stallion Connetable and ridden by Jennie Bullen (now Mrs Anthony Loriston-Clarke, the Olympic dressage rider) who had then recently emerged into adult classes. Desert Storm came out as a 5-year-old in 1959, and she was immediately sensational for her superb presence – as someone remarked, 'She carries herself like an empress!' She won the hack championship at the White City for two consecutive years, although, like most mares, she could have off-days, one of which caused an irate General who was trying to judge her at the Bath & West Show to say that he had not come 200 miles to nag horses!

Soon Desert Storm progressed to dressage and gave Mrs Loriston-Clarke, our most gifted dressage rider, the grounding which has taken her on to international standard.

In 1961 Count Orssich, Ann Davy and Hugh Haldin again had a good team of the large hack Lucky Strike, by The Admiral, bred near South Molton by L. J. Earl and given a good grounding in hunter youngstock classes, and in the small hack Free As Air, by Hot Catch. Both won all the big prizes in 1961 and 1962, and Lucky Strike went on to scale the heights, quite literally, when he joined the Massarella show-jumping stable and divided the puissance at the Horse of the Year Show over some fantastic height. Ridden by Malcolm Pyrah, his joint winner was ridden for Italy by Captain Raimondo d'Inzeo.

The last top hack to be produced by Count Orssich, champion at Richmond and Windsor in 1964, was a spectacular grey Thoroughbred former racehorse who was registered as The Hittite but shown as Cinderella Man. He was so difficult that the peg dropped out before the end of the season, and strong young soldiers were detailed to school him around the showgrounds prior to the hack day, but to little avail.

By the late Sixties and early Seventies David Tatlow had followed on in his father's footsteps and was virtually dominating the show-hack scene, with a good sort of bay mare, Mrs Samways's Lady Teller for the large hack division and Shalbourne Last Waltz for the small division. They were respectively champion and reserve at the Horse of the Year Show in 1970, and in the following year the laurels were accorded, most deservedly, to Right Royal, owned and ridden by Vicki Spencer-Cox from Cheltenham, who had given her national champion a somewhat unusual but clearly beneficial preparation for the Horse of the Year Show by taking him to Pony Club camp for a week in the pony lines. No doubt on returning home he would have taken even Wembley with equanimity! In 1972 he successfully defended his title. By V-Ray, he was bred in Wales and, aged 6, was the hack of the year for consistency too, barring a lapse at the Bath & West where he went up on end. Champion at Royal Windsor and the Royal, he was sold to Mr and Mrs Richard Ramsay before Wembley, where he was ridden by Vera Holden, who had broken him as a 4-year-old.

Shalbourne Last Waltz dominated the small hack classes for the third successive year before retiring to stud.

Robert Oliver was now coming to the fore, and in 1973 he won all the plums, including the Wembley title, on the Hon Mrs David Joly's Young Apelles, a chestnut by Whistler who cost a large sum as a yearling but was not a success on the racecourse. At Windsor Right Royal was shown over-fat, and behaved badly to boot, as he did too at Peterborough, while Young Apelles failed to put a foot wrong and won at the Bath & West, the Royal and Peterborough, although the final Wembley accolade eluded him when Right Royal's connections rallied their forces to take the title for the third consecutive year, then made history by pulling off a fourth victory in 1974, ridden by young Fiona O'Neill, his new owner. The following year he failed to make it five in a row – a record – when he showed every indication of entering the Royal Box backwards and the title went to a small hack, Miss Betsy Profumo's and Mrs William Stirling's Lemington Moon River, who had been beavering away all the season to become far and away the most consistent small hack under Jennie Loriston-Clarke's production. Bred in Northumberland by Mrs Nigel Pease, he was by the TB stallion Comandeer out of the pony mare Prudence, by Gay Presto.

More significantly, Mrs Loriston-Clarke brought out for Mrs Goodall, his breeder, a bay 4-year-old by Tenterhooks called Tenterk whom I described in the 1976 *Horse and Rider Year Book*, which Alan Smith of *The Daily Telegraph* and I edited for eight years, as:

> A most impressive newcomer who seems destined for stardom in 1976, being possessed of great quality, presence, type and temperament. Champion on his first outing, at Devon County, he won the novice class at Royal Windsor and was reserve champion to Right Royal at the South of England. When he reappears he is well poised to take on the established champions.

What impressed me about this 4-year-old at the Devon County, his first public appearance, even more than his elegance, conformation and type was his demeanour. When he was in the ring during the parade of prizewinners he stood stock still and watched with mild interest as the sky became filled with pink smoke, out of which parachutists dropped into the main arena all around him. To be so completely unflappable at the age of 4, he had to go far, and so he duly did. As Robert Oliver so rightly said in his book: 'Champion for three consecutive years at the Horse of the Year Show, his correct conformation, movement and ride made him virtually unbeatable.'

When Tenterk came to the fore there was already a small but select band of top large hacks jockeying for position at the major shows. One was Susan Anne Rose's Good News, also, like Right Royal, by V-Ray, and found by Peter Tozer, a farmer-dealer near Exeter, turned out in a field near Bristol with a herd of pigs – animals that are usually looked upon by well-bred horses with grave suspicion. Tozer was looking for a good hack for a client, Alfred Newbery's daughter Joyce. He telephoned to say: 'I've got good news for you' – and that is how the horse acquired his name. A true hack type, he took both Joyce Newbery and Susan Ann Rose out of the pony classes with consummate success and it was appropriate that on his very last appearance, at the Horse of the Year Show, he should win the large hack class from all his younger rivals. At the start of the season, when three people were trying to buy him, Colin Rose had resisted temptation by giving him to his daughter, and he spent the rest of his life carrying her around their farm in Derbyshire.

But, Tenterk apart, perhaps the most interesting hack of that entire season was Dr and Mrs Gilbert-Scott's Fair Change, by the premium stallion Fair Gledhill, bred on Dartmoor near Ivybridge by Mrs Peregrine Murray-Smith out of a mare she bought at Exeter market. Sold during the winter by Jennie Loriston-Clarke as a dressage horse, only seventeen points short of advanced category, he had been so over-dressaged that his temperament was sadly out of sorts and his new owners decided to show him in an attempt to settle him down. He also went to Mrs Julia Wynmalen for a remedial course with his rider, Carole Scott, and he gradually began to settle down and enjoy his work again.

Shown at Royal Windsor, he went well for his owner but boiled with the judges. The Scotts, nothing daunted, persevered. At the Three Counties Show a month later he went very well and Mrs Beryl Maundrell gave him the championship, which he repeated at Hickstead. But the storm clouds were already hovering and the following week, at the Royal International at Wembley, they broke.

Plate 26 Carole Gilbert-Scott on Fair Change, unbeaten in 1985; Champion Show Hack of the Year; Supreme Champion and Ladies' Champion Hack and Cob Championship; Best-trained Hack of the Year; Champion of Champions at the Horse of the Year Show, after which he retired. He is now turned out with Cusop Pirouette, but is still ridden regularly at the age of 20 (Carol Gilson)

Rumour was rife that the horse had had a chequered career, and that two years earlier, when he was being produced by David Tatlow, he had been 'spun' by the vet and the conformation judge on the concrete for having been fired for a curb. So the judges – one of whom had, in fact, given him the championship a fortnight earlier before the rumours began to get about – regretted that they were unable to judge Fair Change, and he went home to the Thames Valley with his career ostensibly in shreds.

But this would have been to underestimate his owners, who showed him again at Hickstead in August under Mrs Richard Hawkins, with her husband a joint-Master of the Grafton and a very knowledgeable, courageous and determined lady. She had, of course, heard all the rumours and still retained an open mind, examined the hock, realised that there was neither a curb nor the evidence of a former curb and that the horse was sound, and decided that as Fair

Change is a lovely horse and a true hack – a type that is by no means easy to find – he deserved to win. Most people were delighted to see him receive his third championship, but the green-eyed monster is never too far from the showing scene and complaints were made to the British Show Hack and Cob Society, who, via their secretary, Mr John Blackmore, wrote a letter to *Horse & Hound* requesting exhibitors not to show, nor judges to judge, hacks that had been fired for any reason.

What had now become a cause célèbre ensured an unusually large crowd of spectators on the Friday morning of the Horse of the Year Show, when the contenders for the Rochas Parfum Hack of the Year title were assessed by Mrs Harry Hindle (ride) and Mr Archie Smith-Maxwell (conformation). As is the custom at Wembley, all the show classes are split into two for judging of ride and conformation separately. A sizable group was viewing Fair Change's hocks with as little ostentation as possible, but Mr Smith-Maxwell kept them all in suspense as, with admirable sang froid, he started by examining the front end of the horse. Then he moved around to the hind legs, subjecting each seat of curb to exhaustive scrutiny and tactile examination before requesting the opinion of the duty veterinary surgeon, who is always on hand throughout the conformation judging.

The professional opinion was that there was nothing to see or to feel and that the hocks were clean. Thus Fair Change, after a really fair crack of the whip, was named among the nine called in for final judging in the arena that afternoon, and in the event finished second to Good News, thus vindicating his owners' faith in him, and justice was at last done and seen to be done. From then on, Fair Change continued being a hack 'for fun', as light relief from being a serious dressage horse.

The indomitable Mrs Loriston-Clarke, who works so hard with so many facets to her life, brought out another very nice small hack as a 4-year-old, and a home-bred one at that, Desert Storm's daughter Catherston Lonely Breeze, by her Thoroughbred stallion Xenocles, who is also a sire of event horses and has himself competed in one-day events.

When Tenterk's time had come to retire from the ring, Robert Oliver had found another worthy successor in Tomadachi, by News Item out of Merrily and Honour, champion at the Royal International for three years on the trot. More Thoroughbred than

Plate 27 Robert Oliver on Tomadachi, Champion Hack for three years, at the Royal Bath & West Show (Kit Houghton)

Tenterk, with more limb and front, he has been sold into semi-retirement to a very good home. His place has been taken by Rye Tangle, who has now won the Wembley title twice, in 1985 and 1986, once ridden by Robert and most recently by his wife Ali. Bred by Mrs Greenway from Hampshire by Hot Deal out of Lady Catherine, Robert was asked to look at the hack she had bred and, greatly to his surprise, found himself buying it that afternoon. Rye Tangle is now 7 and won the Champion of Champions award.

Robert Oliver, the sole surviving showman who produces and rides champion hacks and hunters with equal panache and success, is a reliable custodian of each, and a dedicated enthusiast as well.

All of the older hack experts, and many younger ones as well, agree that the standard has deteriorated greatly since the pre-war and early post-war years, yet no one seems quite sure why this should be. I thought that Count Robert Orssich, who came to England in the 1930s and has since produced more champions than anyone else, might know the answer. The son of a nobleman who was an officer in the Austro-Hungarian cavalry, he did.

I think it is true to say that there is not, at this moment, an outstanding animal being shown. The top-class hack has always been hard to find, and it always will be, but we saw better animals in the past. It could be because of all this awful Anglo-Arab business, with oriental blood being used more and more. They pass on an ugly and exaggerated tail carriage, bad shoulders – I have yet to see an Arab with a good shoulder – and worse hind legs. The Arab hind leg is an abomination and yet, strangely enough, they never get curbs and nothing ever seems to go wrong with them!

Count Orssich was taught the classical concept of riding by instructors from the Spanish Riding School in Vienna.

One was taught to school a horse on very orthodox lines, which had to be modified for hacks when I came to England. A basis of orthodoxy is a good foundation on which to build, but for the purpose of showing hacks it requires modification to get the essential elegance and lightness in hand which is so often missing in the modern show hack. For example, I consider that every good hack should be capable of being ridden with only one hand – in other words, he should neck rein.

Production nowadays is far too hurried. It takes two years to train and produce a show hack correctly, and today it is rare to find one that has been really well trained. Riders do not seem to work at the essentials – the cadenced and rhythmic walk, trot and canter. Horses are forced into a stilted and exaggerated action at the trot instead of a relaxed and regular 1-2-3-4 movement. This same forced and artificial action is also becoming far too prevalent with the show ponies, who suffer from the same hurried training.

Equitation as such has improved a lot, and most of the people one sees in the show-ring are actually riding fairly well; but the standard of training and presentation leaves a lot to be desired. The single show, for instance, is usually so uninteresting. Why should it not include a half-pass or two, a turn on the quarters, even perhaps a flying change of leg? This is, of course, advanced equitation, and it is not easy to teach a horse to do it, but it is quite possible to achieve if the rider is sufficiently knowledgeable. As it is, the only variation in the single show seems to be of the stupid, gimmicky kind – dropping the reins on the horse's neck, for instance. I long to say to these people: 'For heaven's sake pick up your reins and don't mess about!'

The show hack should ideally be the easiest of all animals to ride – but how many of them are easy? Time after time I have heard the top hunter judges saying: 'I am sorry, I won't come and judge hacks because I cannot ride them.' The true hack should be a pleasure to ride, not a penance. All of my hacks, or almost all of them, came to me straight out of training, and they possessed idiosyncrasies which I had to get rid of before they even went into the ring. Unless the temperament was really wrong it could be done, but it took time. Everything one does in the way of training a horse takes time, and short cuts seldom lead to success.

87

Plate 28 Mrs Robert Oliver on Rye Tangle, 1986 Show Hack of the year (Kit Houghton)

Driving a horse onto the bit and inducing a fixed head carriage, I suggested, was one of the most common faults today, and Count Orssich agreed.

> The head carriage should result naturally from the mode of progression – not by producing a right flexion, then a left flexion, then a right flexion again, and so on. Hurried training and wrong basic principles are to blame here again.

I suggested that the influence of dressage might be having an adverse effect upon the production and training of the show hack, some of which moved like the German dressage horse, considered often, even in dressage circles, to be ugly.

> At least we must not completely condemn the fundamental principles of orthodox riding, but the carriage and movement of the horse must look easier. It must be lighter in hand, with its hocks well under it, and the canter should be more collected but nevertheless easier. The horse should also show obedience to the leg.

THE · SHOW · COB

Traditionally, the high-class cob is supposed to have 'a head like a lady's maid and a farewell like a cook' – or, as Surtees allowed John Jorrocks to express it: 'Those two great twin 'emispheres are among the chief glories of the cob.'

The weight-carrying cob is a general utility animal, and the ideal riding cob is strong enough to carry a 16-stone rider to hounds. Yet he must also be able to gallop, and ride like a hack, which necessitates combining quality with his weight-carrying capacity. He is often considered to be an old gentleman's horse, and many hunting men resort to a cob before the ultimate Land-Rover. At the other end of the scale, young people sometimes go from ponies to an intermediate hunting cob before acquiring a hunter. The cob is also eminently suitable for carrying its owner around the farm, or visiting friends informally, or down the road to the post-box, or exercising the dogs – anywhere, in fact, where it is preferable to ride than to use one's feet, which is virtually everywhere!

The word cob is employed very loosely, and indeed the type, like the hack, is hard to define and impossible to breed to a standardised pattern, other than the Welsh cob, which is an animal with strenuous knee action of the ride-and-drive variety. The show cob is very much a riding animal with good, sloping shoulders, but there are also driving cobs, of the vanner type, which are purely harness animals with a large proportion of plebeian blood in their veins. They may be clipped out, their heels trimmed and they may be masqueraded as riding cobs, but they will deceive only a very few, characterised as they are by underbred heads, straight shoulders and the high action of the harness horse, while the limbs are composed of round, soft, porous bone rather than the hard, flinty bone of the blood horse.

The true riding cob is a heavyweight hunter in miniature, somewhat disguised by a hogged mane. Until a few years into the 1950s they were docked as well, but the Docking and Nicking Act put paid to this barbarous procedure – one cannot imagine how they must have suffered when turned out to grass in the summer, to be eaten alive by flies with no earthly chance of keeping them at bay.

As far as breeding is concerned, the cob is a freak. He is usually by a Thoroughbred or polo pony stallion out of a thickset pony or a butty small hunter mare. The Irish cobs used to be on the coarse side, but in the last decade or so some grand cobs have been bred there, some of the best being a mixture of Thoroughbred, Irish Draught and Connemara pony. The official height limit for the show-ring is 15.1 hands, although for hunting, 15.2 or 15.3 hands cobs are to be found. Their immense character is manifested in their outlook, and in the gaiety and sprightliness of their step. A little blood head, strong back and quarters, great depth, and at least 8in of bone below the knee complete the picture.

The Brothers Young of Melton Mowbray, John and Dick, a famous and respected family of horse dealers, produced the best cobs in England between the wars. Each year at Olympia, with mono-tonous regularity, they won the cob class until they came to be regarded as the uncrowned kings of the cob world. After the last war their place was taken by Mrs Rosemary Cooke of Tetbury. Over more than a decade she showed many cobs, all winners and two of them champions.

The first was Knobby, a grey, old-fashioned sort in a class of his own. The type no longer exists, but it was great. Foaled in 1935, his breeding and background are wrapped in mystery, but Mrs Cooke first saw him at the Boxing Day meet of the Whaddon Chase in 1940, ridden by Phil Oliver of show-jumping fame. She bought him there and then and he worked on her farm throughout the war, mowing, carting and ploughing. When she broke her leg in the hayfield, he carried her home to the doctor, bareback, with infinite care. A brilliant hunter – unridable unless permitted to be in front – he jumped a famous brook in the Duke of Beaufort's country that has stopped any number of big horses, and he won every class at the Beaufort hunter trials in 1946. His first big win at the White City in 1946 was repeated in 1948 and 1949, when he was also Show Cob of the Year at Harringay.

In 1950, when Knobby retired, his owner brought out the chestnut Alexander, who was champion at Windsor on his first outing and remained supreme for the next four years. He retired after winning the Windsor championship again in 1955. In 1952 he was Cob of the

Plate 29 Mrs Rosemary Cooke on Alexander, who stood supreme for four seasons in the early 1950s, before the Docking and Nicking Act was passed by Parliament

Year at Harringay and, like Knobby, he won at Richmond and the Royal and all the leading shows. Bred in Ireland, he was bought from a tinker at a fair for £32, with £1 back 'for luck', by an Irish farmer, who worked him in harness. Every morning Alex left his stable and made his way to the kitchen for breakfast with the family which he ate off the table, so the unlikely story went. His next owner was a Mr Riorden, who paid £42 (£2 back for luck), and then Count Orssich bought him for Mrs Cooke, who started showing ponies in 1922, aged 7.

The third great cob to come from the Beaufort country was Benjamin, who was spotted at a Westcountry show in 1946 by Mrs Pamela Carruthers, now the most famous and travelled builder of show-jumping courses in the world, with over a quarter of a century's top international experience behind her. Benjamin was owned by Mrs 'Pug' Whitehead, who was then Master of the Monmouthshire and hunted hounds off him. She saw him again at the Bath Show, where he was second to Knobby, and got Howard

Dixon, the well-known Chippenham dealer, to buy him for her, before he left the ring.

Bred in Breconshire by Mr Llewellyn Richards of the famous Criban Stud, Benjamin was the last son of the premium stallion Furore and his dam was a pit pony. The week after she bought him, his new owner took him to Cirencester and beat the hitherto inviolate Knobby. She then hunted him, and her Christmas card that year was a picture of him, one of which she sent to Captain Tony Collings at Porlock. Soon after Christmas, Mr Howard Riddell was going to Porlock to try a show hunter and on the way there, held up by the Duke of Beaufort's hounds, he noticed a cob jumping on and off the road. When he arrived at Porlock, he saw the photograph and recognised Benjamin, and was so struck by the coincidence that he made such a large offer that Mrs Carruthers could not refuse it.

Tony Collings showed the cob that year except at the White City, where he was judging hacks, so Mrs Carruthers had the ride and won not only the cob championship but the Winston Churchill Cup for the supreme champion riding horse. During 1948 she continued to show him and in the following spring she bought him back again, when he continued to sweep all before him and won at Windsor and Richmond for the third successive year. Having been loaned for two seasons to the late Duke of Beaufort, who hunted hounds off him, he was hunted by Christopher Carruthers and at the age of 16 he was winning hunter trials, working hunter classes and Pony Club one-day events.

Mrs Carruthers was sent to Paris to forget about horses when she left school in the Thirties, but her mother sent her some money to buy a fur coat and she acquired instead a 2-year-old filly that had run on the flat but was too small for racing. She schooled her in Paris and brought her back to England as a 4-year-old, when she won at Olympia.

The next really outstanding cob, in my opinion, was a wonderful grey fellow called Sport, who won at Dublin with Marshall Parkhill in the saddle and then came to England in the ownership of Mrs Z. S. Clark. He immediately proved himself to be insuperable, and remained so for six seasons in the 1960s winning six Wembley titles. He was judged in Dublin, and put on the road to fame and fortune, by Colonel Sir Andrew Horsbrugh-Porter, who was then hunting correspondent to *The Field*.

The most successful cob showman over the years has been Roy

Trigg, who has found some wonderful patterns and taken them to the top of the tree, having always had a liking for a good cob, and, having the eye that has enabled him to find them in unusual places, has had more than his share of good ones. He always kept a good hunting cob, and for his first cob owner, Miss Baldry, the grey Jonathan and the black Vodka were both adjudged Cob of the Year. Then came Cobber from Cobh, which he found in Co Cork, the brown Justin Time which he showed for Lady Zinnia Pollock and the chestnut Huggy Bear. The latter came, very poor, from Robert Healy-Fenton in Co Wexford, was by the Thoroughbred Golden Gordon and won three consecutive Cob of the Year titles at Wembley.

The present cob in the lovely yard near Billingshurst is Just William, who was also bought in poor condition near Newdigate in Surrey as a 3-year-old. He was called some uncoblike name – P.C. Copperfield, if my memory serves me right – and when the previous owner, who had bred him, discovered that his name had been changed to the much more suitable Just William, she was most irate

Plate 30 Roy Trigg on Huggy Bear, Irish-bred by Golden Gordon (Kit Houghton)

and wrote to the British Show Hack and Cob Association and *Horse & Hound* to complain.

Roy, in the meantime, had sold the cob, by sheer chance, to John Dunlop, the Arundel trainer who was in his yard one day, saw the cob's head over the box door, asked what it was and said: 'I'll have that!'

'Don't you want to see it out?' asked Roy in amazement, for John Dunlop had only seen the head.

'No – he'll be all right if you've got him. I've always wanted a show horse!' – and the deal was done. Luckily, said Roy, the cob won first time out, and his owner was so enthusiastic that he decided to accompany Roy to the Cork Show and look for a heavyweight colt, which they duly bought. Then they went back to the Dublin Show to see how he fared there and bought another. The following year, 1986, the Cork colt won the 4-year-old class at the Royal.

Meanwhile, having bought the cob, Roy and its owner resented being told that they could not change its name because the breeder wanted to advertise her stallion, and took the matter up with the Hack and Cob Association. They argued that hacks who have Thoroughbred names in training have their names changed constantly when they are registered as hacks, and if they can do it, why not cobs, who are not even Thoroughbred? Naturally, they won the day, although *Horse & Hound* still declined to use what was a really good story, I thought, and quite unique too, about a top racehorse trainer becoming an avid owner of show horses.

He really enjoys the shows, especially the one-day agricultural shows in the Westcountry – he goes and looks at the cattle and round the trade stands and appreciates the whole thing. And he loves his cob – he takes him home for the winter and the driver arrived to pick him up. 'What am I taking?' he asked. 'Oh, just an old cob,' Roy told him. 'Good Lord!' he laughed, 'I was sure it was a Derby winner – I've been sent with hock and kneecaps, bandages and tailguard, rugs, the lot!'

THE · ARAB · HORSE

The Arab is the oldest and purest of all breeds, and his blood is probably to be found in every variety of horse in the world. The dry air and soil of Arabia produces horses with more muscle and smaller, denser bones than those of any other breed, and in order to bring harder bone to soft-boned types of horses he has been used to improve many varying species for hundreds of years. He has a unique combination of strength and stamina with lightness, and he has also imparted his speed, his grace and his courage to our native breeds.

There are those who claim that the present-day Arab is a direct descendant of Solomon's stud, and many Arab horse dealers carry papers to prove that this is so. The Bedouin of the interior, however, keeps no pedigrees, for these have been handed down orally from generation to generation, and the breeders known the ancestry of their stock as well as, if not better, than their own family trees. The Arab is generally believed to trace to one or other of five mares on which Mahomet and his four immediate successors fled from Mecca to Medina in the night of the Hejira (15 July, AD622) but, however this may be, it is certain that pedigrees of the Kohlani can be traced for six hundred years.

The first Arab stallion is reported to have been brought to Britain in the reign of James I. Since then, through the male line, he has given us the Thoroughbred, probably the old pack-horse and thence the hackney. The Arabs guard the pureness of their strains very zealously against foreign blood, and they are always reluctant to part with their mares, but their stallions have gone to all parts of the world. The foundation of the General Stud Book of English Thoroughbred Horses, first published in 1791, is based upon seventy-eight Yorkshire racing (Galloway) mares and three Arab stallions – the Byerley Turk, the Darley Arabian and the Godolphin Arabian, or Barb, from North Africa. Nearly one hundred years later, in 1878, Wilfred Scawen Blunt, of Crabbet Park, imported a certain number of Arabian mares, some of which were captured in war while others were bought for fabulous sums – one of them having previously been exchanged for forty-four camels, the sum of £100 and presents worth another £100.

The head of the Arab is his most beautiful and characteristic feature – the 'dished' or concave face and the delicate, tapering muzzle imparting a fine and bloodlike appearance that distinguishes him from all other breeds. The neck is arched and very powerful, with the throat well developed and the chest, although inclined to be narrow, is very deep and the girth considerable.

The shoulders, although also characteristic, are, with the hind leg, the least prepossessing points, and are responsible for the hunting fraternity's (as well as the racing man's, whose preoccupation with shoulders and hind legs is rightly proverbial, and for the best of reasons) dislike of the Arab in his pure state. The shoulders are inclined to be straight, short and upright, so abbreviating his front and making the rider feel uncomfortably close to the front door. The back compensates to some extent by its shortness, while the loins and quarters are extremely powerful. The forearms are long to the knee but the cannons are short, the pasterns long and springy and the feet deep and sound. The tail is set on high, and the Arab perhaps more than any other breed can be said to 'carry both ends'. Colour varies between grey, chestnut, bay and brown, but blacks, roans and broken colours are taboo.

As a racehorse in England the Arab has not been a success, except when confined to the few races restricted to his own ilk. In former years he was matched to run against Thoroughbreds without success, but in India, and in many other parts of the world, many of the best flat horses are pure-bred Arabs, and by our standards they carry big weights over very long distances. As far as the genuine long-distance races are concerned – over distances not of 3 miles on the racecourse, but of 100 miles or more across country, the tests of strength and endurance in the desert – the Arab is out on his own.

The Crabbet Park Arabian Stud, near Crawley in Sussex, founded by Wilfred Scawen Blunt, was at its peak when owned by his daughter, the Rt Hon Lady Wentworth. The family goes back to the leading racing families in England and France, tracing to Charles Martel, AD722, who defeated the Saracens and distributed hundreds of Arabian horses all over Europe. Lady Wentworth herself won her first Grand Championship of Egypt at the age of 15, and bred Arabs throughout her long life. A number of important long-distance races have been won by Crabbet-bred stock, and Champion Crabbet holds the world record for long-distance racing and speed over a distance, as well as for soundness and weight-carrying ability – 310 miles, carrying 17½ stone. In 1919, Champion Ramla, aged 10, won the USA championship race over 310 miles, carrying 14½ stone, and competing against Thoroughbreds, while Kheyra won over 162 miles continuously carrying 14st 4lb.

In the early and middle Fifties, Lady Wentworth had no fewer than fifteen champions in her stud. Supreme Champion Grand Royal, a 15.3 hands chestnut, home-bred, was by Grand Champion Oran out of Royal Centenary Grand Champion Sharima, by World Champion Gold Cup winner Shareer out of Champion Nashisha, was sold for 6,000 guineas. As a 2-year-old in 1949, Grand Royal was a supreme champion, and in winning three grand championships and four supreme championships, beat all the best in England.

The Crabbet-bred grey mare Grey Royal was another supreme champion, by international champion Raktha out of Sharima, thus half-sister to Grand Royal. She won fifteen supreme championships and is especially notable for having been put to the Derby and St Leger winner, Airborne. Their Anglo-Arab filly Grey Imperial won the open mare championship at the Arab show as a 3-year-old. She was one of four champions bred by her dam.

When Lady Wentworth died, Crabbet was run by her daughter, the Lady Anne Lytton, and then by Mr Covey, the manager. The only other breeder to have won the supreme championship at Roehampton in that era was Mr H. V. Musgrave Clark, whose stud was also in Sussex at Offham, near Lewes. He bred and showed Arabs for over sixty years and was a regular exhibitor from 1900. He sold his young stallions for large sums all over the world, and he imported the famous grey pre-war stallion Skowronek, later owned by Lady Wentworth. His famous supreme champion was Bahram, a chestnut horse, 14.3hh, when in training and fit he girthed 73in and had 8¼in of bone. His dam, Betina, also bred at Courthouse Farm, 15hh, is the dam of Boaz, a grey stallion who was exported to South Africa after twice running being the supreme champion at the Breed Show at Roehampton.

Since all this had established the Arab horse in England, for its own sake and not merely as an improver of other breeds, the scene has changed prodigiously in the last thirty years, during which the best Arabs in the world have been found in England. The Arab Horse Society, founded in 1918 to preserve the pure blood already existing in this country and to encourage the introduction of further specimens of the best type, had Wilfred Scawen Blunt as its first president. Since its inception it has issued its own stud book and compiled a register of part-bred and Anglo-Arabs, sponsored flat races for Arab horses at Newmarket and elsewhere, conducted endurance tests for Arab horses, in addition to furnishing information to all parts of the world, maintaining a sales register and inaugurating a premium scheme for brood mares. Not only does it hold an annual show at Roehampton, it also subsidises other major shows which stage classes for Arabs.

Cecil Covey carried on Crabbet until he, too, died and the stud was dispersed. Since then Michael Pitt-Rivers' Salisbury stud has also closed down, but many more have taken their place with many different and improving strains – Polish, Russian, German, Spanish, Italian, Portuguese, American and Australian. The Polish and Russian Arabs have improved the hind legs and the hocks of British stock and their shoulders are also benefiting from the availability of foreign sires.

Plate 31 Major and Mrs P. J. Maxwell's Salomy, full sister to World Champion Arab Siwah

Major and Mrs T. W. I. Hedley have had their Briery Close Stud at Windermere in the Lake District since 1957. The major was born in that beautiful part of the world and his wife went there as a child during the war. She had always aspired to owning a beautiful chestnut Arab mare with a flowing mane, and now she and her husband own ninety-six Arab horses. They went first to Miss Gladys Yule of the Hanstead Stud in Hertfordshire, another of the old-established and best ones, and bought Count Rapello, son of the famous Count Dorsay, who was a great winner both in-hand and under saddle, ridden by Miss Jane Kent, Miss Yule's god-daughter (now Mrs Colin McHugh). Then, again from Miss Yule, they acquired General Grant, and next the Crabbet-bred Orion from Cecil Covey, and so on.

Major and Mrs Patrick Maxwell, who own Lodge Farm Stud at Batcombe, near Shepton Mallet in Somerset, married in 1967, when Mrs Maxwell had been breeding Arabian horses for five years, and thereafter it became a joint effort. In 1973 they moved from their place near Mold in North Wales in order to expand, and they now have 9 stallions (2 leased) and 30 mares of their own, and have leased a Jordanian mare, desert-bred, and a Polish-bred. The three main groups trace back to Bahrain and a desert-bred mare called Nuhrah, another family to Sobha (Crabbet imported her in 1878) and Egyptian and Spanish-bred. The Barb comes from Tunis and Morocco and looks like the Russian AkelTeke breed.

The Maxwells had 22 foals in 1985 and 18 in 1986, and they export to 20 different countries. The Russian Government Stud bought one of their stallions: they export 900 foals annually, 80 per cent of those bred there.

Emma Maxwell, daughter of the house, regularly hunts an Arab stallion with the South and West Wilts, and the Egyptian-bred Fakhr El Kheil has won and placed with her racing, in a one-day event, show-jumping, and also won in-hand at the European Champion-ships. He is highly intelligent and knows quite well that competitive outings, or days with hounds which he thoroughly enjoys, bear no relationship to his stud duties.

Mrs Joan Ratcliff's Claverdon Stud had exported Arabs to many parts of the world, including South Africa, Jordan, Iraq, Saudi Arabia, Belgium, the Netherlands and the USA. Egyptian and Russian-bred Arabs have been imported. In 1983 the stud amal-gamated with the Al Waha Stud in Surrey, the Bohemian Stud at

Stoke-on-Trent and the Water Farm Stud at Ipswich to form Beefeater Farms Ltd, to breed and sell top-class Arabians. They leased the Tersk-bred stallion Klarnet from Dr Lombardi of the well-known Italian equestrian family for 1984; for 1986 the German-bred Narav Ibn Aswan was leased from Silvia Garde-Ehlert to stand at Mrs Bancroft's stud at Ipswich.

Claverdon's successes include a first with their black colt Alaswad in Paris in 1981 and the Junior National title with Zemire, in 1978. Foaled in 1977, Zemire was a champion brood mare, beating good stallions. The stud also bred the grandam and great grandam of the US National Champion, Padron, whose progeny have won world-wide. Racing is another activity, and the Emirate of Dubai contributes substantial donations through the support of Sheik Hamdan Bin Rashid Al Maktoum.

In recent years the registration of pure-bred Arabs in England has been static around the 900 mark. In 1985 the greatest number of horses going overseas went to the Middle East, a trend which continued in 1986. At the time of writing, a large sale of horses is being organised to the government in Algeria, a country to which British horses have not been exported previously.

Arab flat racing under Jockey Club supervision, instigated in 1978, grew to eight meetings in 1986 at venues such as Aintree, Goodwood and Kempton Park, and ten in 1987. The Arab Horse Show at Ascot is probably the largest single breed horse show in Europe, attracting well over a thousand entries.

THE · CHILD'S · SHOW · PONY

The child's pony as we know it today – the marvel and the envy of the rest of the world – has been with us only since the early years following World War II. As far as the general public was concerned, it started in 1945 with the birth of Pretty Polly, who was bred at Kells, Co Meath, by Mrs S. A. Nicholson, by the grey Arab stallion Naseel, out of a Welsh mare called Gypsy Gold.

Pretty Polly was produced in the ring as a 4-year-old at the Dublin Horse Show by Miss Barbara Falloon. She won the championship, and the following May she staged a repeat performance at the Royal Ulster Show in Belfast, when she was sold to Mr Albert Deptford, an East Anglian farmer from March, Cambridgeshire, a well-known breeder of Suffolks. He sent her to Mr and Mrs Keith Lee-Smith of Peterborough to be ridden by their daughter, Davina. Polly was Show Pony of the Year at Harringay and was virtually unbeaten for the next three years, thrice champion at Richmond, the Royal, Peterborough, the National Pony Show and the Royal International at White City, and twice at Royal Windsor and Harringay.

In 1951, Mr Deptford followed up Pretty Polly's purchase by investing in her sister, the hand-smaller My Pretty Maid, who had won at the Dublin Spring Show in 1951. He then had an unbeatable pair for the 14.2 and 13.2 hands classes who wound up with almost monotonous regularity as champion and reserve. This happened in 1951 at the White City and the National Pony Show, while at Harringay My Pretty Maid finished third to her older and bigger sister and full brother, Miss Janet Richardson's Eureka.

Pretty Polly remained unbeaten until the International Horse Show of 1953, when she met defeat at the hoofs of Colonel and Mrs J. F. S. Bullen's Royal Show, ridden by Jennie Bullen. The decision, which caused quite a fluttering in the dovecotes, hinged almost entirely on type. There were those who faulted the Irish pony on her comparative shortage of front, common to all Arabs, which she

inherited from her sire; while others preferred to overlook this discrepancy and put her superlative beauty and quality above the somewhat coarser, more robust good looks of Royal Show, the only pony ever to lower Pretty Polly's colours. A liver chestnut son of the polo pony sire Grey Metal out of the pre-war 13.2hh Olympia winner Flash III, he was bred in Lincolnshire by Mr William Benson. In 1947, he was bought by Miss Sylvia Calmady-Hamlyn of Dartmoor fame, who showed him at the National Pony Show and gave him to Jennie Bullen as a 3-year-old. He won the championship at the Royal Counties, Bath & West and Aldershot three times consecutively and was Pony of the Year at Harringay in 1952.

Plate 34 Gay Coates on her grandmother's My Pretty Maid, Pretty Polly's full sister

Plate 32 Mrs Nicholson's Arab stallion Naseel, who founded a pony dynasty in Ireland with the Welsh mare Gypsy Gold

Plate 33 Davina Leesmith on Pretty Polly, by Naseel, who only once tasted defeat in the ring

In 1954, Pretty Polly's last season, she was shown very lightly, winning the championship at the Royal and then going on to the White City, where her main objective, one suspects – or rather, that of her 'connections' – was to turn the tables on Royal Show, which she duly did. Her career as a ridden pony then ended and she was retired to stud. Her sister, My Pretty Maid, Show Pony of the Year in 1953, remained very much on the scene to uphold the family honour. She was bought in May by Mrs K. V. Coates, who started showing ponies in 1935, and won the Richmond championship in 1938 with Kavora Kismet, ridden by her daughter Anne (who also won the City of London Cup for the best child rider). In 1939 Anne won the Richmond championship again with Kavora Roulette, while her brother John rode Kavora Kismet to win the City of London Cup and then won the championship with her at Olympia.

After the war Mrs Coates had many good ponies with the Kavora prefix – Chips, Dubarry, Tiddlywinks, Graceful, Wendy, My Pretty Maid – and attributed much of her success to the enthusiasm of her stud groom, Mr H. Harries, who had been with her since the Thirties. Her 'jockey' was her grand-daughter, Gay Coates, who won the Windsor championship twice on My Pretty Maid, was supreme at the Ponies of Britain in 1954 and Pony of the Year again in 1955.

We now need to go back in time to the first year of the century, when Elinora Maria (Nell) Gwynne Holford was born at Bwlch, a small village on the hills of Breconshire. Her father, James P. W. Gwynne Holford, was MP for Breconshire from 1870 to 1880 and was the first vice-president of the Welsh Pony and Cob Society. He had inherited his love of horses from his mother, and continually stressed the importance of improving the standard of the Welsh Mountain pony at a time when the stud book was being established, breeding was at its lowest ebb and the standard in grave danger of deterioration. A keen hunting man and a breeder of hunters, he also had some very good driving horses and drove a team.

Nell's mother, awarded the CBE for founding, at Roehampton, the first orthopaedic hospital for officers and men wounded in World War I, was a shrewd and enthusiastic breeder of livestock, in particular pedigree Jerseys, Guernseys and Herefords. She encouraged her daughter to establish a stud of Welsh Mountain ponies, and the Bwlch Stud was founded in 1910. In the early 1920s Buckland, her father's estate, was sold and Nell was forced to leave her lovely home, her beloved hills and her Welsh friends. She moved her stud to her mother's home, Hartpury House, now the Gloucestershire Farm Institute.

When she married Leslie Weaver, a horse dealer in partnership with the late Captain Andrew MacIlwaine until he went to live in Ireland, her life became all hunters instead of ponies. But she started again with ponies by chance when, driving with her husband past Jack Castle's farm in Oxfordshire, she spotted a chestnut mare in a field. This was in 1931 and the mare was Goldflake, who later achieved fame as the dam of the great pony stallion, Bwlch Valentino. By Meteoric (a son of the Derby winner Sunstar), she was out of the flapping pony Cigarette, who was a legend throughout South Wales. Only 13hh, she was never beaten at her height and won a great many races in Carmarthenshire up to 14 hands 2in.

Goldflake had been purchased with a draft of cattle at Llandilo, and Nell bought her for £35. She had inherited her mother's wonderful movement and won a great deal, including at Olympia in 1934, and was champion at the Royal for Mrs Darby. Two years later she fell into bad hands and Nell was able to buy her back at Tattersalls for 100 guineas. She put her to stud during the war, when she lived at Crickhowell and ran the Brecon branch of the SSAFA. From then Nell bred Welsh ponies, and later riding ponies, including the legendary Bwlch Valentino, by Valentine. Not wanting the trouble a stallion entails, she sold him as a 4-year-old to Mr Vivian Eckley, who stood him at his Cusop Stud near Hay-on-Wye, in Herefordshire.

Having acquired Miss Minnette, a mare by Malinen out of old Kavora Kismet from Miss de Beaumont, Mrs Pennell put her to Valentino and bred another grey colt, Bwlch Zephyr. When he became so colty that he was chivying and chasing her Guernsey heifers all over the place, she contacted her veterinary surgeon and made an appointment to have him gelded. Fortunately, her friend Elspeth Ferguson, whose Rosevean Stud near Worcester was extremely successful, rang up and said: 'For heaven's sake let me have him!' It was the happiest solution imaginable, for Zephyr became as famous a sire as his father and the family influence was extended still further with the three brothers, Zephyr, Zip and Zingaree, the latter owned by Colonel and Mrs J. F. S. Bullen.

The next development was when Mr Llewellyn Richards, joint-owner of the Criban Stud at Talybont-on-Usk with his brother Dick, which had been in the family for over two hundred years, gave Mrs

Pennell a wonderful pony mare called Criban Red Heather, by Criban Loyalist (by the polo pony Silverdale Loyalty of Mr Herbert Bright's), out of Criban Heather Bell by Criban Cockade, out of the wonderful old mare Criban Socks (see Plate 45). Covered by Bwlch Zephyr, Red Heather bred Bwlch Hill Wind, a wonderful sire of quality ponies and a great winner in the show-ring himself.

The best of his sons was Rosevean Eagles' Hill, of whom more anon. But as a champion both in-hand and under saddle, the first to make his mark was Albert Deptford's home-bred Gem's Signet, whose dam, Polly's Gem, was a daughter of Pretty Polly by Bwlch Valentino. Gem's Signet stood at Miss Ferguson's stud as a 3-year-old, served a small number of mares and was then gelded, to keep the blood in the right hands, before being sold as a ridden show pony to Miss Amanda Sangan, who lived in Jersey, for the record sum of £8,000.

Six years old in 1973, Gem's Signet continued to win, although only just 14 hands, giving away 2in in height. He was supreme at Windsor, South of England, Three Counties, the Royal, East of England and Royal International, and at the National Pony Society Show at Malvern took his ninth major ridden championship, as well as being champion again at the twenty-first Ponies of Britain Show at Peterborough, first over his ridden brethren and then over all the led stock as well, with his dam standing reserve to him.

His progeny, too, did him proud. His 2-year-old son, Miss Ferguson's Rosevean Signet Ring, was champion 14.2 pony and reserve overall at the National Pony Society Show, and was supreme young pony at the Ponies of Britain with Holly of Spring, also by Gem's Signet, as reserve. Signet Ring went on to stand reserve to his grandam, Polly's Gem, for the led championship.

The alliance which Mr Deptford instigated between the Pretty Polly family and Mrs Nell Pennell's Bwlch strain put this new dynasty at the very top of British breeding. It seemed impossible to imagine any bloodline beating it, and none did. But alas, when Mr Deptford died no one kept the Pretty Polly line going.

The Bwlch line stemmed, through its first male progenitor Bwlch Valentino, from polo pony blood crossed with Welsh. The Pretty Polly line, Welsh again on the distaff side, had Arab blood that was by now sufficiently far removed to allow the displeasing racial characteristics of upright shoulders, bent hocks and lack of second thighs, to be virtually eliminated in the course of some thirty years.

Plate 35 Bwlch Valentino assured immortality for himself and his breeder, Mrs Nell Pennell, when he sired Bwlch Zephyr, who sired Bwlch Hill Wind, who sired Rosevean Eagle's Hill . . .

Plate 36 Bwlch Valentino's most illustrious son, Bwlch Zephyr (Kit Houghton)

Arab blood is invaluable in pony breeding, provided it is well in the background of the pedigree.

Gem's Signet continued to dominate the ridden classes in 1974, but he was vanquished at the Royal International by Dr and Mrs M. Gilbert-Scott's Blythford Chinook, a bay son of Bwlch Zephyr, and at Wembley Chinook was beaten by his stable companion, Christmas Carol of Bennochy, by Lennel Strolling Minstrel. The breeding classes were dominated by Mrs M. E. Mansfield's brood mare Rotherwood Peep Show, a former champion under saddle whose grandam was bought for a mere £100 at an NPS sale, and by Chirk Catmint, a bay daughter of Lady Margaret Myddelton's Section B stallion, Chirk Caradoc. The young stock champions were Albert Deptford's Holly of Spring and the yearling Gem's Kestrel.

Sadly, 1974 saw the death of Mr Vivian Eckley's wonderful riding pony stallion, Bwlch Valentino, at the ripe old age of 24 and still serving a few mares up until his death.

In 1975, just when Gem's Signet, having dominated the ridden show pony scene for four years had retired from the public gaze, his now 4-year-old daughter Holly of Spring assumed the mantle of supremacy that he had just discarded. A chestnut mare by Gem's Signet out of Penhill Finola, a mare bought by Miss Elspeth Ferguson from Mrs Coates' stud at Brixham in Devonshire. She was by Colonel and Mrs Bullen's palomino stallion Bubbly, who was by Mrs Harry Frank's small Thoroughbred Potato, by Tredennis, out of a Bwlch Valentino mare sold by Vivian Eckley to Mrs Coates and out of Finola by Potato. Finola's dam was of unknown ancestry, but Miss Ferguson used to hunt her.

Holly came out at Windsor to win the 13.2 hand class and the championship and was sold to Mr and Mrs C. A. Cooper, sent to Davina Whiteman (née Lee-Smith) to produce, and went through the season unbeaten, at all the major fixtures, the NPS and the PoB. Ridden by 10-year-old Catherine Cooper, she had a lovely floating action and quite impeccable manners, never appearing to have an even slightly mischievous thought in her pretty head.

Miss Elspeth Ferguson made history when she sold Gem's Amethyst for £12,000. The reserve to Holly of Spring at most of the major shows was Dr and Mrs Gilbert-Scott's Arden Vol-au-Vent of Creden, and the little dun Rotherwood Snap Happy, Holly's stable companion, was reserve at the Royal and Newark.

In 1976 Holly retained her invincibility, save at Royal Windsor,

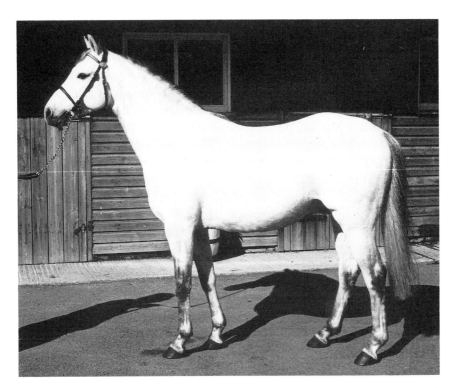

Plate 37 Bwlch Hill Wind, son of Bwlch Zephyr and Criban Red Heather and sire of Rosevean Eagle's hill, a dual Lloyds Bank Champion (Kit Houghton)

where the judges, Mrs William Hanson and Mrs David Bourne, preferred Mr and Mrs J. Milligan's Gay Sovereign, by Gem's Signet out of Gaiety Girl by Gay Presto, (a twin son of Precipitation who did not grow very big), out of a Dartmoor mare. Again the most consistent runner-up to Holly, as well as winning many championships in his own right, was Arden Vol-au-Vent.

The most successful in-hand pony was Miss Elspeth Ferguson's Rosevean Eagle's Hill, a yearling by Bwlch Hill Wind out of the 22-year-old Perdita bred by Mrs Phelps-Penny by Count D'Orsay. After a highly successful season, he covered himself with glory by going up to Wembley and beating all the hunters to win the Lloyds Bank In-Hand Championship for the supreme led horse or pony of the year.

When, in 1978, Holly of Spring won the Show Pony of the Year title at Wembley for the fourth consecutive year, she too put herself among the immortals, as had her sire, Gem's Signet, before her. As for Eagle's Hill, in 1978 he won the Lloyds Bank In-Hand Championship again as a 3-year-old, having served thirty mares in the spring. At the Royal Show he was champion riding pony for the

Shown from Mrs Mansfield's Rotherwood Stud, Wind Flower is actually owned by Mrs S. R. O. White of the Colbeach Stud at Horninghold, Market Harborough, where Downland Mandarin stands. Another resident is Pendley Birthday Girl, bred by Mrs Dorian Williams by Enstone Artist out of Pendley Maypole, winner of the overall British In-Hand Championship at Bucks County.

Dr and Mrs Michael Gilbert-Scott, who live near Maidenhead in Berkshire, have far from given up show ponies, although their three children are long past the stage when they ride them themselves. Carole Gilbert-Scott, who looks after the horses and ponies with her sister, Simone, explained.

> Mum was the original enthusiast. Now we're all involved. Dad, who practises in Windsor, used to sail. Then he came to a few shows and enjoyed them, so he sold his boat, bought a horse-box, and as well as transporting horses and ponies to the shows, it also took 22-year-old brother Andrew to Formula Ford race meetings. After exercising a couple of ponies, I go and help him grind the valves. It's all great fun and a real change. We have no grooms here, and no mechanics either!

The family regard their animals as ponies rather than 'rosette machines'. They all live 'in the garden' – or at least the stable yard in what used to be the orchard, where they have eleven boxes.

> One has ferrets in it! We still have our first show pony, Cusop Pirouette, because we could not bring ourselves to part with her. We also have her four children, some still unbroken, who are simply pets. It's not really economic!

The lovely little bay mare, Cusop Heiress, was one of the best ponies they ever owned. Foaled in 1972, she was bred by Mr Vivian Eckley near Hay-on-Wye, where for twenty years he stood Bwlch Valentino. Heiress is by Cusop Dignity (by Valentino) out of Cusop Hostess. Dignity's dam was Norwood Delilah, who was by the Arab sire Samson out of Edward Crow's old pony Angela, by the Thoroughbred Perion. Heiress was bought as a 2-year-old and sent to the Scotts to break. Later they had the opportunity to buy her. As a 4-year-old she had just four outings without any kindergarten preliminaries. She made her debut – a winning one – at the South of England, then went to the Royal International and finished third to stable companion Christmas Carol of Bennochy, then went to the Horse of the Year Show, where she was second.

The following year she had a few more shows and by the time she

THE · WORKING · PONY

In the pony world there was growing discontent in the early 1970s among those who knew and cared, concerning the discrepancy between ponies who won in the show-ring and those with more bone, substance and a more equable temperament who could reasonably be expected to give a child a good and a safe day with hounds. This led to the increasing popularity of the working pony classes, where the entries, although perhaps without the quality of some of the show champions, but with bone, substance, a calm temperament and, above all, the ability to perform, are matched against others with similar qualifications and expected to give a good account of themselves over a course of fences that look as natural as possible but provide a test for both pony and rider.

The underlying idea originally was to give a chance of winning to the child whose parents could not afford, or did not wish, to buy a top-class show pony for their child. The fact that some would pay four figures – or even eight times four figures – for a 4-year-old gelding was patently ridiculous, indicative of false values and wrong priorities all round, however, rewarding for the breeder. Now, working ponies have caught on to such an extent that prices have climbed rapidly and it is impossible to find a potential winner costing less than £500, and they often run into four figures or more.

Once established, this new enthusiasm spread like wildfire, providing an outlet for ponies who just 'missed it' in terms of the show-ring proper, as well as placing a welcome emphasis upon performance. Important though show ponies are for the sake of the breed, few are suitable to go hunting or give a child much enjoyment, and pot-hunting is by no means the beginning and end, mercifully, of a normal child's ambition. Most top show ponies are in any case too 'sharp' to be ridden in the hurly-burly of the hunting field or Pony Club rallies, quite apart from the fact that they are too valuable to risk over stone walls, banks or bedsteads.

A child neither wants nor needs an everyday pony with the temperament of a Thoroughbred horse, which is likely to take off at the slightest provocation, thereby doing untold damage to his rider's nerve. Courage is one thing, but flightiness is quite another, and regrettably most show ponies are flighty to a degree. By breeding for looks and quality it is inevitable that a placid temperament is sometimes sacrificed, so the child's sense of security is jeopardised. By the time the average child can control a blood pony, the chances are that he or she will have outgrown ponies anyway.

Even an adult who is over-horsed may soon become nervous, and this can happen even more easily to a child. The working pony is a suitable conveyance and will give his rider a great deal more fun than a miniature racehorse who requires to be ridden in and worked by a lightweight adult to remove the fizz before a child can get up. That is why the British show pony is not in demand on the Continent. The native pony, particularly Welsh, Dartmoor and Connemara, with the better-looking New Foresters, find a ready market in France, Germany, Italy, Holland and Belgium. Although some show ponies have gone to the United States and to South Africa, Australia and New Zealand, they are really bred for the British market. Much as the foreigners admire them, they do not wish to buy them for their children. The Welsh Section B pony, particularly, which averages 13 hands 2in, is eminently suitable, and Lady Margaret Myddleton has for many years bred a strong type of Section B pony at her Chirk Castle Stud in Denbighshire, while her stallion Caradoc is the sire of many show-ring winners.

It is still by no means unusual to see a judge overlooking lapses of manners in the show-ring, and following the form book by turning a blind eye to these misdemeanours. But handsome is as handsome does, and a pony enjoys a working class and gets rid of any inhibitions at the same time – without getting rid of the child. The child will enjoy taking it to Pony Club rallies too, and riding in a junior one-day event or a hunter trial, instead of swanning around in a navy-blue coat with a plastic rose in his or her buttonhole.

Working ponies were first classified at Badminton and called working hunter ponies. Prices have gone rocketing up from £500 or so to £2,000, such is the demand for a working pony that knows its job or shows potential, but it is surely money better spent in terms of a child's enjoyment and safety. With the emphasis increasingly on performance, and the tremendous, ever-increasing popularity of the three-day event that is so admirably suited to the British and Irish horse with riders who have a history of foxhunting and riding across country, the working pony is the natural forerunner to the event horse for those of the young entry who are competitively inclined.

By 1975, the Ponies of Britain Show, so wisely directed by its founder, Mrs Glenda Spooner, was staging not only working pony classes but also in-hand classes for young working ponies. These provide a showing outlet for yearlings to 3-year-olds with no pretensions to pulchritude but commanding a far wider market. They have also encouraged breeders to improve the native mares and produce animals with more bone and substance. Andy Croft produced some splendid ponies, ridden by his step-daughters, Jane and Wendy Dallimore. Coalport, by the premium stallion Sashway, was supreme champion at Peterborough, the Royal and Windsor for the third successive year, and the hand-smaller 13.2hh Rusty, bought in Hereford market for the proverbial song, won many championships, while Little Dominic stood supreme at Oakham, the National Pony Society and Kent County.

Show pony classes really require professional production and a 'professional' child rider, who forgoes the counter-attraction (if such it can be called) of academic endeavour from May to October in order to follow the show circuit, which they may regret later on. But the working pony, a performer first and foremost, does not have to be stabled, can be turned out in the field during term time, does not require daily exercise, and can well adapt himself to working in the holidays if adequately fed at grass, especially if he is to be hunted. A barn in the field with a trough and one of those excellent hay racks surmounting a wooden manger for feeds will serve the purpose admirably, and a New Zealand rug will permit trace clipping, though of course the pony will be cleaner and more comfortable if brought into the stable.

As Mrs George Gibson, joint-Master of the Cottesmore Hounds in Leicestershire, so rightly says:

> Rich parents can't just go out and buy a super pony, get their child taught to ride it and then, hey presto, it wins every championship, because it is part looks and part performance that wins, so it's a real leveller. It can never be cut and dried, as a show class can, and so hope can spring eternal in the children. As long as the pony is well made and jumps well it can afford to be a little less than elegant – its own natural talent, as well as that of its rider, will make sure that it has a good chance of doing well.

119

Working hunter pony classes have now been going on for years – they were held at Badminton when Prince Charles was riding 13.2 ponies – but they needed standardised management, so Mrs Gibson has been administering them for the British Show Pony Society, of which she is chairman, since 1968, and they have gone from strength to strength.

> We now go from the Cradle Stakes, for the very smalls, just off the leading rein, to large children with 15-hand animals who can pop round bigger fences. The tinies start at one-foot-nothing. And in 1979 for the first time we had classes for led working ponies at the Ponies of Britain Show. It has all caught on tremendously and the young ponies are really good sorts. For the children, it's like Aintree, Badminton and Cheltenham rolled into one and the most important thing each spring is to qualify for Peterborough. It is Mecca to them all – and the experience they gain can take them on naturally to eventing or show-jumping or working hunter classes, so it is really a class with the future in mind.

Mrs Joanna McInnes, whose stud at Spofforth, near Harrogate, is the home of the celebrated brood mare Whalton Ragtime and Lennell Strolling Minstrel, a stallion still active at 25, is very keen on the effects of the working pony classes, which she considers give two great benefits to participants – that of giving the children a different dimension in their riding and making them ride a great deal better, as well as encouraging 'proper ponies' at the expense of those without either sufficient bone or substance, too many of which have been bred in the misguided attempt to produce a champion with four crosses of one pony stallion in two generations.

Major Eric Worthington, who lives near Wellington, was *chef d'equipe* of the British working pony team for the British Show Pony Society team for several years from the time the international championships started in Ireland in 1976, shepherding his charges to Bavaria twice, to Denmark and on several occasions to Ireland, where they are particularly keen. In 1985 the BSPS held its last event in Scotland, at Scone Palace, where teams competed from Germany, the Netherlands, Belgium, Ireland, Scotland and Wales, as well as Great Britain. Countries very interested but unable to make the journey then, although they hope to in 1987, were the United States, France, Italy and Jersey.

They are all, Mrs Gibson tells me, particularly interested in our working hunter pony classes and were very impressed by the strong, rustic courses built over here, as well as the type of pony (children's *real* hunter type) competing in these classes. Over the last two years new classes have been instigated which are an instant success, for the show hunter pony is extremely popular. The type is middleweight hunter with quality, and they must gallop on. The side-saddle ponies come into the same category and are a lovely sight. Ponies should be slightly longer in shape but of great quality, and with impeccable manners.

As I write, in January 1987, plans are now afoot for the next international event, at the Newark and Nottinghamshire show-ground at Winthorpe from 19 to 21 July. Teams to have signified their intention of competing are from Sweden, Italy, Germany and Belgium, with Ireland, Wales and Scotland from nearer home. The teams will consist of four riders on ponies of 13, 14, or 15hh, to contest a working hunter class, dressage and show-jumping, and it is certain that the ponies will enjoy it just as much as the children.

BRITISH · NATIVE · PONIES
Mountain and Moorland

THE WELSH MOUNTAIN PONY (Section A)

The Welsh Mountain pony, who still lives in a comparatively wild state on the hills in Wales and the Border counties, is indisputably the most beautiful of all the native breeds. He is also ageless, and his forebears have roamed those self-same haunts since prehistoric times. The 'Araby' look of the Welsh head, with its concave outline, is often erroneously believed to be a fairly recent characteristic, owing to the fact that Arab stallions have been enlarged on the mountains during the last hundred years; but this is only partly true, and research has revealed that an Arab-like appearance was a distinct characteristic of the Welsh Mountain pony long before any deliberate attempt was made to improve his quality. It is, indeed, virtually established that the eastern blood was assimilated from the pack-ponies brought to the British Isles during the Roman occupation and abandoned when their owners were routed in AD410. The Roman legions had previously equipped themselves with horses in the course of their African campaigns.

The typical Mountain pony does not exceed 12 hands in height, for the bigger pony would not survive the rigours of a winter on the desolate heights. It is big for its height, however, in the way of depth and width, and is possessed of prodigious strength and stamina. The head is small, breedy and intelligent, wide between its bold eyes, and the face is 'dished' or concave, ending in a neat little muzzle embellished by distended nostrils. The jowl is prominent, and the ears small and thick and firmly pricked. The line of the throat is clean, the neck supple and fairly cresty in the stallions, and the shoulders are well laid back. The back is strong across the loins, and the tail is set high and carried proudly. Well-sprung ribs, a deep girth and full quarters complete the body, and the limbs are short, with flat bone and big knees and hocks. The mane and tail are silky, and the pony, although full of quality, is tough, virile and supremely active.

The Welshman may be grey, roan, chestnut, bay, dun, cream, brown or black, but more than a dash of white pigmentation is not correct. Wall eyes are not uncommon but are not, on the whole, popular with breeders. His blood is to be found in hacks, hunters, polo ponies and children's ponies, and it would be safe to say that every hackney pony stallion that has made a name at stud during the past eighty years runs back, frequently more than once, to Mountain pony blood.

Miss Margaret (Daisy) Brodrick, of Abergele, started her famous Coed Coch herd of ponies in 1924 at the suggestion of her stud groom, Mr John Jones, who was still doing a full day's work when he was over 80 and was, Miss Brodrick used to say, 'the brains of the whole outfit'. His grandson, Shem Jones, assisted him for twenty-five years and became chief showman until Miss Brodrick died, when he went to Colonel Edward Wynn. Great-grandson Wyn Jones, then aged 4 (when I wrote the first edition of this book thirty years ago) and shaping well, being already capable of leading a pony, amply fulfilled his early promise.

Plate 43 Miss M. Brodrick's Coed Coch Siaradus, Champion Welsh Mountain Pony Mare (W. W. Rouch & Co)

Coed Coch Siaradus, a grey mare foaled in 1942, was the most famous pony of her day, having won over 50 first prizes and 35 championships, including supreme at the Ponies of Britain Show in 1954 and 1955, and reserve in 1953, from nearly 600 entries. At the National Pony Show she won the Lord Arthur Cecil Cup for the best Mountain and Moorland pony in 1950, 1951, 1953, 1954 and 1955, and she was champion WMP at the Royal from 1951 to 1955. She was by 1955 the dam of 8 foals, 3 of which died, 2 fillies were retained in the herd and 2 more, Coed Coch Sirion and Coed Coch Sulwen, were exported to New Zealand and the United States respectively.

Miss Brodrick bred Siaradus' father (Coed Coch Glyndwr), mother (Coed Coch Sirius) and grandmother, and the great-grandmother was one of the herd's foundation mares. Sirius was sold because she had wall eyes, but in 1941 when Miss Brodrick was home on leave she saw her and offered her owner, Mr C. Lloyd Lewis, a free service to Glyndwr. The result was Siaradus. Mr Jones

Plate 44 Miss M. Brodrick's Champion Stallion, Coed Coch Madog (W. W. Rouch & Co)

saw the filly as a 2-year-old and wrote and told Miss Brodrick that she was a good one and asked if he should buy her, which he eventually did, together with her full sister. Her first big win was the WMP championship at the Shropshire and West Midlands Show in 1950, and in her whole career she was only five times lower than first; then she was second or third.

Coed Coch Madog, who was foaled in 1947, was bred at the stud, by Coed Coch Seryddwr, by Glyndwr out of Coed Coch Mefusen, by Glyndwr, and since the Three Counties Show at Gloucester in 1951, where he won the WMP championship, he was only twice out of the first two at major and local shows. He won 25 championships, 7 reserves and 41 firsts, was 5 times male champion at the Royal, 4 times at the Royal Welsh and in 1955 won the championship for Mountain and Moorland stallions of any breed at the Ponies of Britain Show.

The seventy-odd ponies in the herd lived 1,000ft up on the hills, winter and summer, except for their first year, and were given hay only when snow was on the ground; otherwise they fended for themselves. All the best colts and fillies were retained, and as a result of this policy the stud was able to set its type, contributing to its success in considerable measure.

Perhaps the greatest Welsh Mountain pony mare of all time was little Criban Socks, bred in the Thirties by Mr Llewellyn Richards and sold to Miss Sylvia Calmady-Hamlyn as a 6-year-old in about 1937. She won everything she could at the National Pony Show at Islington and bred three foals in Devon during the war, one of them the well-known show pony Peter Pan, which National Hunt trainer Fred Rimell bought for his daughter, Scarlett. Criban Socks was unfortunately destroyed during the war when Miss Calmady-Hamlyn had to cut down her stud. No one was more disappointed than Lady Wentworth, who had bred thirty-one champion Welsh Mountain ponies and would have given any money for her.

When Miss Brodrick died she left her ponies to Colonel Edward Wynne, with the proviso that when he died all ponies over 18 should be found good homes or else put down.

One of the most renowned and influential studs breeding Section A ponies over the last fifty years has been the Revel Stud of Mr Emrys Griffiths, near Talgarth in Breconshire. It was founded by him and his father in the Twenties, who bought in ponies from Mr W. S. Miller's Forest Lodge Stud at Brecon, Tom Jones Evans' Grove Stud

Plate 45 Criban Socks, owned by Miss Sylvia Calmady-Hamilton, bred by Mr H. Llewellyn Richards and a famous Section A mare

Plate 46 Revel Cello, winner of the 2 and 3-year old colts class, and Youngstock Champion at the Royal Welsh Show

at Craven Arms in Shropshire. In those days, Section A ponies and Welsh cobs were part of the farming scene.

Emrys Griffiths was at the Revel (which means a blacksmith's shop at the junction between two high roads) until moving to nearby Glannant three years ago where he has 10 acres and keeps 3 stallions and 10–18 mares. 'I am still looking for a better pony!' he claims, adding that he would rather lose with a good pony than win with a moderate one. 'I think one learns more from losing than winning.'

Revel is a very illustrious prefix, and one of its most famous bearers was Revel Choice, by Vardra Sunstar, a mare bought from the late Matthew Williams of the Vardra Stud, Church Village, near Pontypridd, Glamorgan. She bred Revel Cassino who was very influential, Revel Chip who died with Mrs Thompson in Suffolk, and Revel Cello (Mrs Gadsden) – all grey and all full brothers by Clan Pip. Bred by the late Mr A. R. McNaught, Revel Crusader was a half-brother to the three stallions, whose dam was Revel Choice.

THE WELSH PONY OF RIDING TYPE
(Section B)

The Welsh pony is bigger than his Mountain cousin, being officially allowed to attain the height of 13 hands 2in, and he falls into two distinct types – the cob pony or Section C (a compromise between a Mountain pony and a Welsh cob) and the pony of riding type. The riding pony is built on bloodlike lines and evolved from a Mountain pony mare and a carefully selected Thoroughbred or Arab stallion. Extravagant knee and hock action are discouraged, quite obviously, and freedom and extension are very evident in all paces, while the Welsh pony gets his toe out in a trot, gallops like a racehorse and is a brilliant natural jumper. Many breeders are devoting their attention to the production of this type of pony, who is already to be seen in great numbers in the show-ring, and has been since the end of World War II.

The first champion Welsh riding pony was Mrs E. G. E. Griffith's grey mare Coed Coch Silian, foaled in 1947, standing 12.3hh and bred by Miss M. Brodrick, from whom Mrs Griffith bought her as a foal. By Tan-y-Bwlch Berwyn out of Coed Coch Seiran, she had an outstanding career as a brood mare, starting at the Royal Welsh Show in 1950. She also won there in 1954, and was champion in 1952 and 1955. She won at the NPS Show in 1952, 1953 and 1955,

Plate 47 Lord Kenyon's Criban Victor, Champion Welsh Pony at the 1956 National Pony Show

at the Shropshire and West Midlands, 1953–5, and was champion at the Royal in 1954 and 1955. In 1956 she was champion brood mare at the NPS.

Silian's first foal, by the polo-pony sire Gay Presto (by Precipitation) won at the NPS Show. Her next four foals, all by Lord Kenyon's Criban Victor, consisted of Verity (who won at the 1953 Royal, was champion at the Royal Welsh in 1953 and 1954, and was exported to the United States); Valiant (also a great winner, as a yearling and at the NPS in 1954 and 1955; was exported to South Africa); Vanity (unbeaten in the show-ring; sent to the USA); and Vesta. After breeding horses all their lives, Mr and Mrs Griffith turned to Welsh ponies after the war at their successful stud at Plasnewydd, Denbighshire.

Lord Kenyon, a director of Lloyds Bank and chairman since 1963 of the Welsh Pony and Cob Society, was formerly a foxhunter with Sir Watkin Williams-Wynn (The Wynnstay Hounds), but when his eyesight became too poor to continue hunting he decided, rather than let grass grow in the stable yard, to breed Welsh ponies, in which he had inherited an interest from his mother. Starting in 1946, he developed the Gredington Stud at his family home near Whitchurch, which is now being demolished three hundred years after it was built.

One of Lord Kenyon's first stallions was the red roan Criban Victor, bought as a 3½-year-old in 1946, when he little imagined how great a champion he would become. A pony of true Welsh type, he was one of the best natured stallions imaginable and so kind, both in the stable and out of it, that even a child could manage him. He was always handled by Gordon Jones, whose father, John Jones, was Miss 'Daisy' Brodrick's stud groom when she started the Coed Coch Stud in 1926.

Criban Victor sired many good ponies and was himself a consistent champion in the show-ring; at the Royal Welsh in 1947, 1958–60 and in 1964; at the Ponies of Britain Show in 1959–62 and 1965–6; and at the National Pony Show in 1956, 1959 and 1960. At the ripe old age of 25 he was Section B champion and reserve supreme champion at the North Wales Association Show at Caernarvon. Five years later he developed an arthritic shoulder and was put down for humane reasons.

Coed Coch Glyndwr, whose influence upon the breed is comparable to that of the legendary Dyoll Starlight, also exerted considerable effect upon the Section B pony through his grandson, Criban Victor. Glyndwr was grey, and the roan pigmentation came from his grandam, Florence. It still obtains to this day and Glyndwr's sons Ceulan Revolt and Farnley Sirius were both red roans. Glyndwr spent the 1939 season at Criban, on an exchange basis with Mathrafal Tuppence, where he sired Criban Winston. In 1943, as Miss Brodrick was abroad on war service, he was sold to Lady Wentworth, who had long been anxious to acquire him, but he left sons and daughters in plenty at Coed Coch.

When Lady Wentworth closed down finally, for the third time, her Welsh stud, Glyndwr went to the late Mr McNaught, father of Mrs John Mountain of the Twyford Stud, remaining until 1953 and adding progeny under both Clan and Twyford prefixes, all of which he stamped indelibly. Ultimately he went to his last home, Miss Marguerite de Beaumont's Shalbourne Stud, and continued to sire lovely ponies until he died in 1959.

Coed Coch also bred Section Bs from its earliest days, based on the celebrated Tan-y-Bwlch Berwyn, who died there in 1953. The Section B herd was dispersed in 1959 but rebuilt afterwards by Berwyn's son, Coed Coch Berwynfa, out of Berwyn Beauty. Outcrosses were made to Criban (H. Llewellyn Richards, the oldest stud in Wales), Downland (Mrs Cuff), and Revel (Mr and Mrs Emrys

Plate 48 Lady Margaret Myddleton's Chirk Curigwen, by Chirk Caradoc out of Gredington Bronwen. A big winner as a yearling, 2 and 3-year-old, including Champion Welsh and Pony Breeding Youngstock at the Royal Show in 1967. She also won under saddle, and as a brood mare

Griffiths). Under a plaque of Welsh slate in the garden of Plas Llewellyn, Daisy Brodrick's home and later that of Colonel Edward Williams-Wynn, lie her beloved hunting pony, First Flight, her companion for twenty-six years, and Tan-y-Bwlch Berwyn, a beautiful Welsh pony stallion, noted sire of many prize-winners, both of whom died in 1953 at the age of 29, and Champion Coed Coch Siaradus, 1942–62. They are described as 'Faithful and dear friends of D.B.'. The inscription reads 'The air of Heaven blew between their ears'.

With Tan-y-Bwlch Berwyn, Criban Victor had the greatest influence on Section B ponies, with the possible addition of Lady Margaret Myddleton's Chirk Caradoc, of whom more anon. Victor was got by Criban Winston (a son of Glyndwr) out of the Section A Criban Whalebone, by the Section C cob Mathrafal Broadcast, who was hunted by Dick Richards before being exported to the USA for use on polo pony mares.

The Lady Margaret Myddleton, whose stud at Chirk Castle, Denbighshire, has made such an impression on Section B ponies, points out that many people seem to believe that Section B (not to exceed 13.2hh) is a recent introduction.

This is not so, as all four sections, A,B,C and D can be found in the index to Volumes I to XVII of the Welsh Stud Book. The Welsh Part-Bred Register is of more modern origin, regulations for entry requiring not less than 25 per cent of registered Welsh blood from sire or dam, or cumulative from both. A study of the early stud books shows, for example, that Eiddwen Flyer II, foaled in 1888, is registered as Section B in Volume I. Dilham Confidence, foaled in 1886, was registered B in Vol III, and no doubt many more can be traced.

In the early 1950s Welsh Mountain ponies had captured the imagination of the general public with their enchanting appearance and lovely action. The other three sections seemed to have lapsed from favour, so that there were very few Bs left, and little demand for them. This was probably true of the cob sections too, though to a lesser degree. Few shows had classes for Section B and these were poorly supported, so I and some of my colleagues sponsored classes at shows to try and encourage interest. Then, suddenly, Section B became the fashion and everyone wanted to get on the band wagon, but where to get them? A number of mares were allowed into the appendix of the Stud Book as FS (Foundation Stock), FS 1 and FS 2 which were quite out of type and should never have been approved. The resulting population explosion of all shapes and sizes of pony gave Section B a bad name which it has taken years of careful breeding to eradicate.

Fortunately, there were a certain number of good stallions to tide breeders over the crisis, so that today one can enjoy seeing large classes of excellent ponies from Section B at all the major shows. Probably the most influential stallions of the late Fifties and the Sixties were Criban Victor, foaled in 1944, his son Coed Coch Blaen Lleuad foaled 1953, sire of Chirk Caradoc (1958) and Chirk Crogan (1959), both out of Chirk Heather, a Victor mare, and Coed Coch Berwynfa (1951), Downland Dauphin (1959), Downland Chevalier (1962), Solway Master Bronze (1959) and Brockwell Cobweb (1960).

Mention must also be made of an FS mare, Silver, bred at Whitchurch, which came into the possession of Lord Kenyon at the Gredington Stud. She was the dam of Gredington Bronwen, Lady Margaret Myddleton's foundation mare who was the dam of Chirk Heather, dam also of Gredington Milfyd who was the dam of Gredington Tiwlyp, the foundation mare of the Rotherwood Stud, and of Gredington Lily, who won so much for the Gredington Stud. Through Chirk Crogan her influence spread to the Weston Stud and later, when Crogan was sold to the Seaholm Stud, she continued her influence there. Seaholm Fritz, by Chirk Crogan, must be one of the best of the young stallions today. Through Chirk Caradoc and Chirk Crogan she has descendants in

Australia, Canada, Holland, Belgium, Denmark, Switzerland, and Germany.

Caradoc was a great personality and a tremendous show-off. He got the most lovely foals, often from quite undistinguished mares, and his progeny groups both in the riding pony and Welsh sections won several times at the NPS Show. He lived to be 25 years old and received admiring visitors from all parts of the world when his progeny had been exported. Perhaps his greatest claim to fame is as the sire of riding ponies. There was Rotherwood Peepshow, immensely successful under saddle in the 14.2 hands classes and later champion brood mare at the NPS and elsewhere. Then there were the three lovely daughters of the TB mare Kitty's Fancy, herself only 14.2hh and the only offspring of a very old mare. By Caradoc she started a family at the age of 14 which included Chirk Catmint, 13.2hh, champion foal at the NPS and a champion from then on, Chirk Caviar 14.2hh, a big winner under saddle and now winning as a matron, then Chirk Cattleya 13.3hh, who won under saddle (including side-saddle) and as a brood mare, and whose daughter Chirk Windflower by Solway North Wind was the 1986 winner of the Lloyds Bank Supreme In-Hand Championship.

Another great moment for Caradoc was when his daughters won all three height classes for brood mares at the Ponies of Britain Show at Peterborough. A Welsh mare, Nantcol Arbennig was first 12.2hh, Catmint first 13.2hh and Cattleya first 14.2hh, with Catmint taking the championship. Lady Margaret will always remember Mrs Yeoman's voice as she announced the result – she loved Caradoc.

When Heather died, before Crogan was weaned, she was found to be carrying a colt foal by Coed Coch Berwynfa. That might have been terrific. Mrs Mairi Borthwick, trying to comfort Lady Margaret for the loss of the mare, said that it was not only a tragedy for her, but for Wales.

The late Mrs Inge, whose father she followed as Master of the Atherstone, was used by Siegfried Sassoon (after hunting there the season before World War I broke out) as the model for Mrs Oakfield of Thurrow Park in *Memoirs of a Foxhunting Man*. 'As well as at Thorpe Hall in Staffordshire, she also lived at Tanybwlch and bred the famous Tanybwlch Berwyn, always keeping a few Section B ponies there.' She hunted when she was 84 years of age, always riding side-saddle in a top hat and with a bunch of violets in her buttonhole, and in extreme old age she used to ride one of these ponies around the garden and park. When she gave up breeding ponies she gave the nucleus of her stud to Miss Daisy Brodrick, of Coed Coch, along with much good advice.

She was a wonderful judge of horses and ponies besides being one of the finest horsewomen to ride to hounds that Lady Margaret has ever seen.

Although a tiny lady, she often rode large hunters which strong men found it hard to control. She knew it was not enough for a pony to have large eyes and small ears if it does not have the excellent conformation which alone can give it the beauty and freedom of action that all Welsh ponies should possess.

It is fortunate indeed that quite a few studs kept some good B mares – Craven, Downland, Cusop, Kirby Cane, Kipton, Sinton were some of them – and the revival of Section B owes them much . . .

THE WELSH COB (Sections C and D)

The Welsh breed of cobs has been established for many years on a standardised basis, although it was originally cross-bred, deriving from a Welsh Mountain pony and a harness animal. From its pony ancestry it inherits its soundness, hard constitution and pluck, and its quality head and ears, while there is much of the pony in its dashing, active trot. The Welsh cob is plentifully supplied with silky tufts of hair on its heels, and the texture of mane and tail hair is soft and silky.

The cob varies in height from 14 to 15.1 hands, and the colour range is varied too, although an abundance of white is not popular and piebalds and skewbalds are not true Welsh colours. He has plenty of bone, which is dense and hard, and showy action which involves considerable bending of the knees and hocks. In former days he was bred for trotting races as much as for work, and the cob Comet, who was foaled in 1851 and owned by the father of the late Tom Jones Evans of Craven Arms, Shropshire (one of the most renowned 'pony men' of all time), trotted 10 miles in 33 minutes with 12-stone up.

Foreign governments, who hold the Welsh cob in high esteem, have taken a heavy toll of promising young sires in the past for breeding army horses and commercial stock. Gaiety and a zest for life are inherent in him, as are stamina and weight-carrying capacity, and the strong back and quarters for heavy work are also there. He has his own stud book, and many of the registered mares, crossed with Thoroughbred stallions, have produced very useful hunters.

Champion of all Welsh cob stallions in the Forties and Fifties was Mr A. Dylan Thomas' Llwynog-Y-Garth, a 15 hands dark chestnut, foaled in 1944 and bred in Montgomeryshire, by Mathrafal out of Melinrug Bess. Bought from Mr Rosco Lloyd of Llanybyther, he was first produced at the Royal at Shrewsbury, where he won. Subsequently he did likewise at all major Welsh shows – in-hand, in harness and under saddle, in addition to siring many winners. He won over 350 first prizes, including eight championships at the NPS. 'Dyl' Thomas' father started the Grange Stud at Neath, Glamorgan, with heavy horses and cobs, his son continuing with premium stallions and cobs.

Miss Ann Wheatcroft started with Welsh cobs in 1954, when she was living with her parents just south of Bath. When her father died she decided to work with horses as a living instead of a hobby, but her introduction to the breed was entirely fortuitous. She read an article on Welsh cobs by Miss Barbara Saunders-Davies of the Llanarth Stud, which she ran in partnership with Miss Pauline Taylor until 1962, and bought, unseen, a 3-year-old chestnut filly who duly arrived on the train one evening. Soon afterwards she bought Llanarth Rhys, then a foal, as a future stallion. She showed him at the Ponies of Britain show at Ascot when he was only 2, and was somewhat disappointed when she overheard Mr Eddie Griffith saying to Mrs Nell Pennell: 'The colt which will go furthest is the one that finished third.' This was the mighty Llanarth Brummel.

Coincidentally, she was just putting Rhys away when she was called for on the public address system to meet Mrs Glenda Spooner, the organiser and brain behind the Ponies of Britain, in the secretary's tent. When she arrived there she discovered that John King, Master of the Belvoir Hounds (now Lord King, Chairman of British Airways), wanted to buy Rhys. She sold him, but bought him back again as a 5-year-old – and bought Brummel, who is now a supreme champion and sire of champions. This 15-hand liver chestnut-roan stallion was unbeaten under saddle and retired from the show-ring, having won every prize for which he was eligible.

When she was building up her stud she was often tempted into selling her best stock in order to make the place pay. But she also bought some outstanding animals, among them the 14.2 hands Palomino, Gelert ap Braint, champion at the PoB stallion show, Kelso, the Royal Highland and under saddle at the NPS. He joined the stud in 1963 and remained until he was 9. Llanarth Claribel was a very good mare who was shown under saddle before being sold to Mrs Nubar Gulbenkian and doing well in double harness.

Without doubt the best ever to stand at her stud, after the Llanarth Stud was left to the University College of Wales, was the black Welsh

Plate 49 Llanarth Flying Comet, Welsh section D cob (Leslie Lane)

cob stallion Llanarth Flying Comet. Trotting as explosively as his namesake, he won the Lloyds Bank In-Hand Championship in two successive years, 1979 and 1980. Sadly, he had to be put down towards the end of 1986, at the age of 18, as he was fading away because his kidneys were failing. Happily, Llanarth Lloyd George will carry on where he left off and he is only 5 years old and also black. There is also Llanarth Solo, son of Llanarth Brummel, to help keep the flag flying.

There is an annual intake of from 60 to 100 visiting mares, some 40 of them registered Thoroughbreds in addition to a number of hunters. The stud has a reputation for getting difficult mares in foal, which attracts owners of shy breeders. The late Colonel Ivor Reeves was a firm believer in the Welsh cob cross a couple of generations removed, and won in the show-ring with hunters thus bred. From 30 to 40 registered cob mares also arrive each season, the stud having won the Ponies of Britain premium for the best Welsh cob stud in England for many years.

Plate 50 Peter Jones's Menai Furious, section C stallion, at Northleach Welsh
Pony Show

Cobs and cross-breds have been exported to Austria, the USA,
Belgium, France and New Zealand, and there is a thriving Welsh cob
stud in Austria, at Maria Anszbach, just outside Vienna. The cobs are
prized as sensible riding horses and as an outcross for Thoroughbred
horses.

The Section C cob, with a height limit of 13.2 hands, is becoming
the latest enthusiasm for breeders, and an extremely popular stallion
is Menai Furious, a *multum in parvo* who stands at Peter Jones'
Menai Stud at Pantydefaid, Llandyssul, Cardiganshire. Both he, his
father Menai Fury, his grandam and his great-grandam have been
bred at this stud, which goes back to 1913. Tom Jones Evans came
originally from Newcastle Emlyn, 9 miles from Menai, where he
stood the illustrious Bleddfa Shooting Star and Ilwyn Cadfor.
Shooting Star covered Clettwr Polly in 1913 and produced Menai
Queen Bee, who was put to Caradoc Llwyd and produced one of the
élite mares, Menai Ceridwen, the dam of Menai Fury, a tremendous
cob-type pony who sired Synod William and the mare Catrina and
Furious. A bay 4-year-old with four white socks and a star, he was
champion of the breed before Christmas 1986 at Olympia.

This is the same female line that produced Menai Sparkling Lady, who won the Royal Welsh at 2 and 3 years of age and was second as a 4-year-old. Menai is the only stud which breeds all four sections of Welsh ponies and cobs, and Peter Jones considers that the Section Cs are challenging the Section Bs as a real family pony.

> Furious has a wonderful temperament. Jim Meads saw him hunting all day when he came to photograph the Vale of Clettwyr the other day, and when two foals were let out I rode him up to the field where someone had put them and they followed him home. He is corned up now for the stud season, but it makes no difference to his disposition, which never alters in any situation. He loves his hunting, too, and stays out until hounds go home.

THE CONNEMARA PONY

The natural habitat of the Connemara, Ireland's only native breed of pony, is the bogs and mountains that lie to the west of Loughs Corrib and Mask, bounded on the west by the Atlantic and on the south by Galway Bay. For centuries he has survived on the sparsest herbage – bracken and bog water constituting his staple diet – and weathered the relentless ocean gales that blow in from the Atlantic.

It is said that rich merchants in Galway imported Arab stallions 300–400 years ago, some of which escaped to join the local herds of ponies which ran wild on the mountains. But not until 1900 was much interest taken in the Connemara pony by any but the local people, who used him for a variety of utilitarian purposes.

In 1923 the Connemara Pony Society was formed, under the auspices of the County Galway Committee of Agriculture, to preserve and improve the breed. Thoroughbred and half-bred stallions had hitherto been allowed to breed indiscriminately with the native pony, but the new society decided to improve the breed from within. To this end, they secured the best available native blood by selecting a hundred mares for foundation stock, and the Department of Agriculture made a grant for the purchase of stallions. Three years later a stud book was compiled and the annual show and sale inaugurated at Clifden, Co Galway, where nowadays upwards of five hundred animals change hands each year at prices which sometimes attain considerable heights.

As a result of this selective breeding policy, the present-day Connemara is a very useful animal – sure-footed, as are all Mountain and Moorland ponies, fast, intelligent and a good jumper with courage but an equable temperament. Compact and deep bodied, he is short backed and well ribbed up, standing on short legs with good bone, nicely sloping shoulders and a well set-on head and neck which give him a natural balance. He varies from 13 to 14hh, with an upper limit of 14.2hh, and more than half of the registered ponies are grey, with blacks more numerous than either bays or browns. Dun was a very typical colour in former years but is today a comparative rarity, and chestnut is not regarded as a typical colour.

There are today several thriving Connemara studs in England, two of them formerly connected with three-day eventing at the highest international level. Most famous of all is the stud near Chepstow, at Itton, started after the war by Mr John O'Mahoney Meade, father of Olympic gold medallist Richard Meade and former joint-Master of the Curre hounds with Fred Broome, the father of another Olympic medallist, show-jumper David Broome. Further north, in Herefordshire, Mrs Stephen Philp keeps the stallion Sean of Leam at Peterchurch, and to the south, near Cranborne in Dorset, Mrs Gordon-Watson has bred some grand ponies from her foundation mare, Silver Lining, whose dun grand-daughter, out of Fortune II, Prosperity of Catherston, was ridden by yet another Olympic team gold medallist (in Mexico on Our Nobby in 1968), Jane Bullen (now Mrs Timothy Holderness-Roddam).

High on the southern fringe of Exmoor, some 700ft above sea level, another post-war pioneer of the breed, Miss Pamela Forman, started her Connemara stud when she left the FANYs after the war, determined to 'get back to the horse'. She went to Ireland and paid £28 for her original grey mare, Cluggan Dolly, who bred four foals and lived until she was 20. Miss Forman now has the fifth generation from this good mare, and with all the interest and enjoyment she and her progeny have provided she must, by any criteria, represent an outstandingly good investment.

The most recent representative of the family is Cluggan Drama, an 8-year-old bay mare by Huckleberry Finn, who stood near Warminster but is now in Australia. She is very typical of the old-fashioned sort of Connemara who hunts and does everything. Cluggan Dolly, her great-great-great-grandam, was by Silver Pearl, and her daughter, Delight, was by John Meade's Lavally Rebel, who was foaled in 1935 and won the Royal Dublin Society's medal on three occasions. In his youth he was regularly driven in a side-car to meet the boat from the Aran Islands to the mainland, taking

Plate 51 Connemara Leam Bobby Finn (Leslie Lane)

passengers many miles across the mountains to the nearest bus route. He was brought to England in 1950 and sired many winners in Ireland and this country. By Rebel, by Cannon Ball, he was out of Derrada Fanny. A famous contemporary was Susan Barthorp's Heather's Own, foaled in 1938, by Noble Star out of Golden Heather, 13.2hh and bred by Mr Laurence McDonagh, running wild until she was 8, and believed to have bred two foals. In 1946 Lady Carew picked her out of a group of ponies being driven along the road. She was very wild, but Lady Carew broke her in six weeks and sold her to Mrs Glenda Spooner at Dublin that year. Then Miss Barthorp bought her and started showing her both ridden and in-hand, and hunted her with the HH. She was twice champion Connemara at the Ponies of Britain Show and once at the NPS.

Mr and Mrs Meade took their mare Finola of Leam, a daughter of their daughter's mare Teresa of Leam, over to Ireland to put her to Carna Bobby, and the result was Leam Bobby Finn, who is as famous in Connemara circles in England as his full brother, Cusheen Fina, is in Ireland. A tremendous model of the Irish stamp of Connemara pony, last year he and his progeny were third for the second time in

139

the Ponies of Britain all-breeds rating. A multiple champion at the Breed Show, he also won the Merlin Cup for the Mountain and Moorland championship at the Ponies of Britain Show, the NPS Show equivalent, and at the West Midlands Stallion Show and the Kelso Show. As his owners have retired, he is now with friends in the North being used on their own mares. Although 20 years of age, he is in very good order.

THE DARTMOOR PONY

The Dartmoor pony, small, hardy and indisputably of riding type, must be a distant cousin of the Welsh Mountain pony, for the Welsh Celts are as the Cornish, if the tales of the early land bridge between Dartmoor and Wales are true. The Dartmoor resembles a bantam-weight hunter, teeming with quality and the courage that can only be associated with blood. Although his limbs, in particular the hocks, are not of the best, crossed with a small Thoroughbred he can and often does produce champion polo and children's ponies.

For all his quality, he is tough and he needs to be, living thousands of feet above sea level on wildest Dartmoor, weathering gales from the Channel to the Atlantic and the Bristol Channel and deriving his sustenance from the barren, rock-strewn moor where the ponies, cattle and sheep, not to mention the rabbits, leave the sward as smooth as a tennis court even in summer. A race of small ponies has existed on Dartmoor since earliest times, and have been used by farmers and smallholders to ride over their grazing lands. Before being superseded by car or Land-Rover, they often took the farmers to market as well.

The typical pure Dartmoor is from 11.2 to 12 hands high, with excellent shoulders and small, erect ears – the ultimate test of pure blood, of which they are the trademark. Traditional colours are bay, brown, black and grey, with an occasional chestnut, and varieties of dun are also seen, although they tend to be rare nowadays. No white markings are allowed, other than a tiny star on the forehead, and a skewbald or piebald Dartmoor is not a Dartmoor at all, but a mongrel half-Shetland animal, the result of Shetlands being turned out on the moor to produce pit ponies. This policy has resulted in a decline in the quality of the animals that roam the moor, and the purity of the breed continues only because the better-known breeders have guarded their stock most jealousy.

Miss Sylvia Calmady-Hamlyn, president for many years of the Dartmoor Pony Society, has done more for the breed than anyone living. Eighty years ago, with no previous knowledge and with 12 acres of land and exactly £30 to invest, she started to breed polo ponies, her ambition being to try to beat Sir John Barker's famous stud. This she succeeded in doing with her one home-produced pony, who won the Duke of Westminster's Cup for the best ridden 4-year-old pony at Roehampton in 1912. This pony played in the last international match before World War I. In 1939 her polo-bred filly was champion at the Royal and won the RASE's Centenary Gold Medal, which is only awarded once every hundred years.

Before the last war her stud consisted of 110 ponies, all hand-picked – polo, riding, Dartmoors, Welsh and Shetland. She was ordered to reduce it to ten ponies, and she saved only the Dartmoors. In 1914 she had taken a Dartmoor pony called Junket from Yes Tor to London, and won the Lord Arthur Cecil Cup – the first time it was offered – for the mare most likely to breed a riding pony. Junket bred the champion Richmond and Royal Show hack Syllabub, which Lady Hunloke (Mrs Philip Fleming's mother) showed. From the same strain came her black stallion Jude, foaled in 1941 and probably the most outstanding Dartmoor of all time. He had an unbeaten career of firsts and championships at the National Pony Show, the Royal, the Bath & West and Devon County, and in 1951 and 1953 at the NPS he won the Shalbourne Cup for the champion Mountain and Moorland pony of all breeds and the Princess Margaret Trophy. In 1951 he spent a week at the South Bank Exhibition in London's Battersea Park (200 miles from home) as a guest invited to celebrate the Festival of Britain, accommodated in a glass-fronted box with tapestry curtains, much to his surprise. Daily he was taken in a horsebox to Hyde Park for a walk, where he evinced much interest in the horses of the Life Guards! Later, he was invited to the Horse of the Year Show at Harringay, which he also enjoyed, entering the arena to the strains of 'Widecombe Fair' and lining up next to the Drum Horse.

Jude had five stallion sons to his credit, and, in addition to many other prize-winning stock, Jenny VII, foaled in 1947 and seventeen consecutive championships. Her first two foals were both champions.

In 1955 Mrs M. J. Gould of Nutcombe, Lustleigh, paid £5 for two Dartmoor pony suckers at Ashburton Pony Fair to eat her grass. Bred

Plate 52 The Dartmoor pony –
Miss Calmady-Hamilton's
multiple champion stallion Jude

Plate 53 Boveycombe Redwing
(by Boveycombe Leo), winner of
the Country Life Cup in 1980,
with Christopher Maude up

by Mr Mann of Widecombe, by Silver Dollar, they could be registered on inspection if true to type, which Pat Robinson (now Mrs Joe Palmer) decided they were. One was Fudge III, who was destined to become the dam of Boveycombe Leo.

Mrs Gould and Miss Calmady-Hamlyn became friends. Both Miss Calmady-Hamlyn and Jude were advancing in years and she decided to give the pony to her new friend, on the condition that he lived a natural life and ran with his mares, and that when Mrs Gould acquired a good colt by him he should be humanely dispatched to his Maker by a local Westcountry hunt. But he lived for four happy years with his little family, his permanent wife Fudge III bore him four children, two colts and two fillies, and as well as Boveycombe Leo he sired another dynasty-founder, Elizabeth Reep's Shilstone Rocks Windswept, the foundation of her stud at Widecombe.

Leo was broken to saddle and to harness, and enjoyed doing odd jobs around the place, but – as is usual in Devonshire, as we found with Bwlch Hill Song, our riding pony stallion – he did not get sufficient mares until he went up to Mr and Mrs Bob Rigby at Bolton, where he was in great demand.

When Miss Calmady-Hamlyn saw him as a foal, she was delighted and said: 'There's your future champion!' and he in his turn has bred champions too, to carry on the line.

THE EXMOOR PONY

The Exmoor pony, which is the descendant of the native British wild horse (the type the Ancient Britons rode), is our only aboriginal native pony, and has been preserved in its old form from earliest times until the present day. Possibly the cold, barren moors, swept by gales from the Bristol Channel, have helped to keep the breed pure, for it is doubtful whether a mongrel pony would have survived the constant exposure to the elements. He is endowed with tremendous powers of endurance, as well as great courage and strength. Despite his small stature (12 hands 2in for a mare and 12.3 for a stallion), he can carry a grown man all day without ill effect, whether across the moor to see to the sheep and cattle or following hounds.

The most important characteristic of what is claimed to be the oldest of all breeds is, for distinctive purposes, his mealy muzzle, and this mealy colour extends under the belly and inside the thighs and forearms, as well as around the eyes – which are termed, locally, 'toad' eyes, being large, wide-set and prominent. The head is on the long side, with a wide forehead and deep jaw. His chest is deep and wide, his back broad and strong and of medium length, and his loins immensely powerful. A well-laid-back shoulder signifies his qualifications as a riding pony and that he is inherently sure-footed. His legs are clean and short, his feet hard and well formed.

The texture of the Exmoor's coat is unlike that of any other native breed. Springy and harsh, in winter it carries little bloom, but the summer coat is short and hard and shines like brass. The suckers have a short, woolly undercoat in their first year of life, and a top coat of long, harsh hair which serves as a waterproof. The colour is brown, bay or dun, no white markings being permissible.

The pure-bred Exmoor is valuable foundation stock for breeding up polo ponies and hunters, and they invariably pass on their tough constitution. Zoedone, who ran first, second and fourth in the Grand National without a fall, had as his thirteenth dam in the tail-female an Exmoor pony, and many of the hunters who cross the moor so well with the Exmoor and Dulverton West Foxhounds and the Devon and Somerset Staghounds have a strong infusion of Exmoor blood. A very useful small cart-horse is also to be found on the hill farms of Exmoor, bred up in three generations from the native pony.

The general farming depression after World War I hit Exmoor particularly hard, and many of the ponies were sold for meat at a nominal price. During World War II many more ponies went the same way, and many breeders were compelled to sell out all their stock. Fortunately, a few well-known breeders hung on to a stallion and a few mares, and thus the breed just escaped extinction.

The Exmoor Pony Society now receives an annual grant from the Racecourse Betting Control Board, and is thus able to award premiums to stallions and subsidies to brood mares, so that the principal herds have increased and new ones have been started. The herds run on the moors all the year, and at the end of October they are rounded up and the suckers, who have been born in May and June, are inspected before being branded.

The Exmoor stallion Heatherman, a champion each time he was shown, won a first premium for many years in 1953. Heatherman, owned by the late Mr S. Westcott, was bred by the late Miss Lillo Lumb, and was by the champion Crackshot out of Heatherglow. The Exmoor mare Greengage was a champion as a 2-year-old filly of the reformed Acland herd (Sir Thomas Acland had the famous original herd in the early 1800s) of Miss R. Green of Dulverton. Greengage, who was foaled in 1953, was shown only once in 1955, when she won the Cheddon Fitzpaine Cup for the best of all breeds at the show out of 111 entries.

The Exmoor was once smaller than the Dartmoor pony, but his height is believed to have been increased by a mysterious dun stallion, built like a well-bred cob, who appeared from nowhere and became an almost legendary figure on Exmoor, where he was known as Katerfelto. Believed to have been the survivor of a shipwreck, he was eventually caught and served several mares in captivity before escaping again and disappearing as mysteriously as he had arrived.

The modern Exmoor has somewhat less bone than his predecessors, but the best are still very good, and the most successful at the present time is Mrs Jackie Webb's stallion Dunkery Buzzard, who was bred from Miss Lumb's Herd 78, which is now managed by her niece, Mrs Vince of Timberscombe. Mrs Webb started with Exmoors by accident, having first bred hunters. She has now been breeding them for twelve years, has twelve at present and has bred her first crop out of Exmoor mares by a Thoroughbred stallion. She hopes thus to breed 'chasers eventually. Coincidentally, Miss Lumb's

Plate 54 Mrs J. Webb's Exmoor pony stallion, Dunkery Buzzard

ambition was to breed three-day event horses this way, and she was inspired by the late Captain Tony Collings of Porlock, who won the second-ever Badminton in 1950 and trained the first British civilian three-day event team for the Olympic Games at Helsinki in 1952, to initiate such a breeding programme. Sadly, it foundered when he was killed in a jet crash while flying out to Johannesburg to judge at the Rand Show a few years later. Miss Lumb soldiered on alone to achieve the third cross. They had reached 15 hands 2–3in, but their bone was disappointing, and they had become somewhat plain of their heads.

Exmoors were immortalised by 'Golden Gorse', on whose splendid books Moorland Mousie, Older Mousie and others published under the *Country Life* imprint I was brought up on in the 1930s. She was a wonderful public relations officer (unofficial) for the breed, and so was Jennie Bullen, now Mrs Loriston-Clarke, who had a marvellous Exmoor called Skipper. I once accompanied her hunting with the Cotley when she was riding him, and on him I saw her tying with two 16-hand horses for first place in the Cattistock *open* Hunter Trial when she was about 10 or 11. Piglet, on whom Rachel Hunt was second at Badminton in 1986, is one-eighth Exmoor, and they are strongly built, with courage to burn. Recently they have taken to driving classes with the same enthusiasm that they contribute to all they do.

THE SHETLAND PONY

The diminutive Shetland, or Zetland pony, is probably the most widely renowned of any pony in the world. He is certainly the most famous of the British ponies, many thousands of young riders having commenced their careers on him, although he is inclined to be too wide for a small child and in fact resembles a miniature Draught horse. He existed in the Shetland Isles long before the earliest records were kept, and in 1568 was described by a chronicler as 'no bigger than an ass, but very strong and enduring'. The crofters used him as saddle and pack-pony, and one of his jobs – the task of the donkey in Ireland – was to carry loads of peat and bring seaweed in from the shore to fertilise the land. Not until 1847 were there any roads in the Shetlands, and wheeled vehicles were almost unknown, so the ponies were put to most transport jobs and worked very hard. In the spring, before the grass came, they were often reduced to eating seaweed to exist, and mares usually only foaled every second year and kept their foal by them for two winters. Breeding was haphazard, and instead of culling the worst ponies, the crofters would sell their best ponies and retain the undesirable ones for breeding.

When, around the middle of the last century, ponies were first used in the pits, a great demand sprang up, and in twenty-five years only yearlings could be obtained. They cost between £11 and £13 a head. When the islands were practically denuded of ponies, Lord Londonderry established a stud on the islands of Bressay and Noss in 1870 to supply his own pits. He and his assistants procured most of the best mares and secured Jack, an outstanding stallion who turned out to be the cornerstone of the stud. Ponies were fairly closely inbred and the bad ponies relentlessly culled, until the present-day show-ring standard was set and fixed for all time. In 1890 the Shetland Pony Society was formed, and Jack and his sons and grandsons are all registered in the first volume of the Stud Book. Nine years later the stud was dispersed, but the groundwork for an improved pony was well and truly laid – with as much weight, and as near the ground, as possible. Practically all the show ponies of today are descended from the Londonderry Stud. In 1892 the Highland Society first staged Shetland classes at its annual show.

Since then the Sheltie has had lean days – the stock was badly depleted from 1911 to 1914, when five hundred ponies were exported to the United States. When the mines became electrified and ponies were no longer required as carriers, the demand dropped so that many people gave up breeding them, while others crossed their mares with other breeds to produce a bigger pony, but fortunately a few staunch supporters stuck to their guns and guaranteed the continuance of the genuine Shetland. His foundation colour is black, but brown and bay are also very common, grey and dun and chestnut are known, and piebalds and skewbalds are mostly seen in circuses. The height limit is 42in at the wither, but the average is 39in, and the smaller ponies are of little use, while the bigger ones lose their breed characteristics. The head should be as small and as short as possible, carried high, with neat little ears, a small muzzle and wide nostrils and eyes. The neck is arched and powerful, the barrel deep and round, the shoulders sloping into well-defined withers, the quarters broad and the tail set high and carried well. The coat is characteristically dense in winter, with long, hard hair growing through a thick, furry undercoat.

Plate 55 W. G. Shillabeer's Wells Three Star Shetland stallion

Mr J. E. Kerr of Harviestoun, Dollar, Clackmannanshire, who was one of the most successful exhibitors of Shetlands, started his stud in 1910, and won the supreme championship at the Royal Highland ten times (1935–7, 1939, 1948–50, 1952, 1954–5) and seven times at the Royal (1939, 1948–50, 1952, 1954–5). His stud supplied many winners also in the hands of other exhibitors, and many of his ponies have been exported to Canada, the United States, the Argentine, Sweden, West Germany, Singapore and Australia. His stallion Beechdair of Harviestoun was twice champion at the Royal Highland and the RASE, while Harviestoun Pat, a charming little mare, was champion at both Royals in 1955.

Now the most successful stud is that of Mr and Mrs W. G. Shillibeer, based not in the Highlands but on Dartmoor, near Postbridge. Originally a breeder of Dartmoor ponies, he and his wife became interested in the Shetland in about 1947, when he came out of the RAF and bought two unregistered ponies which they showed at Chagford and Widecombe. Their interest in the breed increased and in 1954 they bought a mare, Kirkbride Lovely Night, from Colonel Houldsworth. Although Mr Shillibeer has now kept ponies for more than sixty-five years, he knew little about the breed and his new acquisition was a much better mare than he thought, winning at many local shows and standing second at the Bath & West in 1962. They were unlucky in breeding from her, however, for she produced only one filly which they lost with equine flu.

Mr Shillibeer joined the Shetland Stud Book Society in 1954, served on the council for sixteen or seventeen years and had the honour of being president in 1981–2. In 1987 he is President of the Dartmoor Pony Society.

> As time went on we learned a bit more and decided to try and breed a few good ponies. We knew what we wanted and have stuck to the same type of pony ever since. In 1962 we bought a well-bred filly foal, Wells Evora, from the Wells Stud. Three years later we bought a 2-year-old colt, Wells Promotion. He just suited Evora and she produced some super fillies including Lakehead Emma, Emva and Evette. In 1968 we bought another well-bred mare, Melody of Luckdow, and the well-known stallion Wells Three Star, the sire of Evora. I used him on Melody and Evora's daughters and the offspring were all show ponies. We had quite a run of success with these ponies; in 1976 Emma was champion at the Royal Highland, the RASE and the Royal Welsh. She had previously been champion at the RASE in 1969. Also at the 1976 Highland Lakehead Magic Charm was junior champion, Lakehead Melanie reserve junior and they won the Best Group of Ponies. Magic Charm has had a long list of wins including three times champion at the Royal Bath & West.

Lakehead Emma, herself a big winner, has also produced some outstanding ponies. Her first colt, Lakehead Double Brandy, was only shown four times but was RASE champion twice and junior champion at the Royal Highland in 1980. He died unfortunately of internal trouble. Her next colt, Lakehead Double Diamond, was champion RASE 1984 and reserve 1983. He was followed by Lakehead Doublet, who went to four shows in 1986 and was Supreme Light Horse at local shows. She also produced Lakehead Emerald, one of the best show mares who has won a number of native pony championships. Lakehead Evette is another good pony, not often shown, but stood second to another Lakehead pony, Ensign (the champion) at the 1980 Royal Highland. Lakehead ponies have won the Royal Highland championship (a 1,000-mile round trip) and the RASE championship six times, the Royal Bath & West and the National Pony Society seven times, and ponies have been exported to Holland, France, Sweden, Barbados, Brazil and Australia. They keep thirty-head, with a herd of Galloway cattle, and attribute their success to adhering to a sound breeding policy.

THE NEW FOREST PONY

Probably the least wild of the native breeds, his habitat being not only close to human habitation but intersected by main roads carrying a constant stream of heavy traffic, the New Forest pony conforms less rigidly to a standardised type than any other native breed, although certain typical characteristics have emerged and established themselves.

The New Forest has long been a dumping ground for unwanted stallions. In the Middle Ages it was the custom for reigning monarchs to present their counterparts in other countries with a choice stallion, and the kings of England have, at various times, been presented with more such animals than they knew what to do with, so the horses were set free in the Forest. Marske, sire of the famous racehorse Eclipse, was among them. Some improved the breed, while others did just the reverse, and a hundred years ago the New Forest pony was held in little esteem, being coarse about the head, ragged of its quarters and generally mongrel in origin. Eventually, verderers were empowered to control the stallions turned out there. In 1852 Queen Victoria lent them the grey Arab stallion Zorah, and to this day many of the ponies owe their eastern heads to his influence.

From 1891 onwards the verderers inspected the stallions before allowing them to be released. In 1893 Lord Arthur Cecil, in a somewhat original effort to improve the breed, purchased a whole stud of ponies from the island of Rum and also imported stallions from the Highlands, the Cumbrian Fells, Exmoor, Dartmoor and the Welsh mountains, and at the 1914 stallion show there were nine Welsh, five Dartmoors, four Highlanders and three Exmoors among the 121 entries. It speaks volumes for the influence of environment that the Forester has assimilated this heterogeneous selection of blood, while nature has seen to it that the resultant pony is one fairly level type that is best suited to the Forest. Possibly a thousand ponies remain in the New Forest throughout the year, with a further three hundred turned out for summer grazing.

Sir Berkeley Pigott, Bt, founded the New Forest Pony Society in 1938, and it continues to hold a stallion show at Lyndhurst each spring and an August show for brood mares and young stock at Burley. Where accommodation is available, the champion stallion is turned out in a field with a limited number of registered mares. This

150

method of improving the breed from within has been attended by notable success.

The Forester varies in height from 12 to 14 hands. Any colour is permissible, other than piebald or skewbald, although bays and browns predominate. He still has a largish head, somewhat short neck, good shoulders and depth through the heart, although his quarters are inclined to be narrow and drooping. His good action is induced by picking his way across bogs, through high heather and over rabbit warrens from the day he was born.

The champion stallion in 1986 was Mr Owen Dibdin's bay 6-year-old 13.2hh Beechwood Comet, bred by the Hon Mrs Rhys of Burley and sold to his owner as a weaned foal of 6 months. He is one of two stallions, the other being his 3-year-old son. Comet has won numerous championships from a yearling upwards. He was not shown much in 1986 as his owners felt they needed a break, so it was a great thrill when, on his one occasion in the ring, he became champion at the Breed Show and his yearling daughter, Ashley Elena, won the filly class. He has become a good riding pony and enjoys

Plate 56 Beechwood Comet, New Forest Champion at the West Midlands Stallion Show (Stuart Newsham)

being ridden in the Forest. He also likes being schooled, though he finds concentration difficult at times. Mr Dibdin has had New Forest ponies all his life and his wife has been associated with them for the last twenty-five years.

The current champion brood mare is Mrs Fiona Stephens' Brownie of Amberslade, foaled in 1969, winner in 1986 of the Champion Brood Mare and Champion Pony Born on the Forest. She ran out until she was 2, and changed hands twice before Mrs Stephens saw her in a field with her first foal and was able to buy her as a 4-year-old, then in foal to a Thoroughbred. They halter broke her and started showing her locally, quietly progressing to larger shows. She was champion on many occasions, and supreme and reserve champion Mountain and Moorland pony. Her record of winning the New Forest brood mare class for five consecutive years is probably unique.

She has had eleven live foals, nearly all of which have won in the show-ring. They love to jump and have won and been placed in hunter trials, show-jumping and working-hunter classes. Three have run in the New Forest point-to-point, held on Boxing Day across the open forest, two of them winning and the third carrying his breeder to take the special rosette for the first Forester to finish in the Veterans' Race.

Brownie lives out all the year round and detests being stabled, except to get away from the flies in summer. Her 1986 foal, Woodfidley Soft Chorus, was champion foal at the Breed Show.

THE FELL PONY

The cold, rough fells of Cumberland, Westmorland and Northumberland are the natural habitat of the Fell pony, who is very similar to the Dales pony but can boast more quality, and is a better riding type, with sloping shoulders to keep a saddle in its rightful place on steep hills. Like his cousin, he too is a direct descendant of the carrier ponies that carried lead from the mining districts in the north end of the Pennines and the Lake District to the smelting places, and thence to the sailing ships in the Tyne, Wear and Tees. Until ninety years ago, indeed, the two breeds were one and the same in all but name.

The Fell pony's primary function was the carrying, loose-headed, of ore over the rough tracks of the North Country hills, and when

Plate 57 Border Black Empress, by Waverhead Rambler, owned and bred by Mr Clive Richardson, Honorary Secretary/Treasurer of the Fell Pony Society. Winner at the Royal Show, at the Ponies of Britain (Peterborough and Kelso) and the National Pony Show twice. She was four times ridden champion at the Breed Show (Leslie Lane)

not thus employed he was entered for trotting matches, which were the great sport of that time. Trotting matches were featured at the agricultural shows in the district as show-jumping is today, and the big shows would put up a first prize of as much as £40, but pony trotting died out with the incursion of American-bred trotting horses from Glasgow and Manchester and their attendant retinues of bookmakers. In the 1850s the Welsh trotting cob Comet did a great deal to improve the breed, and some years later Mr Gibson's Mountain Heather became the most famous of Fell ponies.

The Fell Pony Society was founded eighty years ago, and five £80 stallion premiums were awarded by the Board of Agriculture, and later by the Light Horse Breeding Department of the War Office, to encourage the breeding of sturdy 13.2–14 hands weight-carrying ponies. The Fell Stallion Show was held each April at Penrith, and the standard became so high that Fells would go down to the National

153

Pony Show at Islington each March and sweep the board. In the year that Fell ponies won all three cups (stallion, brood mare and group) the first Fell stallion was sold to Spain, and thereafter the Spanish Royal Commission returned time and again for Fell stallions, which were also exported to the Argentine, the United States and India. In 1933 the Light Horse Breeding Department ceased to function, as with mechanisation the horse had become redundant, and the society without its premiums was in a parlous state until King George V heard of its plight and offered a King's premium that enabled breeders to keep going. King George VI also stocked his deer forests and grouse moors with Fell ponies, and the Queen, when Princess Elizabeth, drove her Fell pony mare Linnel Gipsy to victory at the Royal Windsor Horse Show in 1945.

Black Fell ponies are the most numerous, and also the most popular, but dark brown, bay and an occasional grey and dun are also to be found. The Fell looks very strong, hardy, and alive, with exceptionally good legs and feet, and he carries much fine, silky hair on his legs and even on his jaw. The shoulders are long, sloping and well set back, and the neck is fairly lengthy and gives a good outlook and front. The chest is strong and the girth deep, the loins extra strong and the quarters equally so. The disposition is kindly and tractable and the pony is an all-round family animal that can be ridden with equal pleasure by an 8-year-old or by his grandfather. In recent years a breeding enclosure scheme has been adopted and it has been extremely successful.

Mr James Bell of Caldbeck took over from his father and started on his own in 1946, trying to improve their stock wherever possible. He and his father have both been very successful in the Fell pony world but his grandfather preferred and bred heavier horses. His father bred Fells for a long time before he ever bothered about registering them, which few people did fifty years ago, but now everyone is trying to be fashionable. His two daughters both ride and drive, and have driven the best mare, Waterhead Magic, who started breeding at 20 after nine seasons' driving. No pony had more championship wins – for four successive seasons she was overall champion both in-hand and under saddle. Of her 6 foals, the first 2 had the wrong blood groups and they lost them both, but they have her 3-year-old son, who has been kept entire, and a 2-year-old filly, Magic II, as well as 7 brood mares and 2 stallions. They have 10in of bone and although the height has been raised to 14.2hh, they have tried to stick to the old-fashioned 13.2hh type. The Dales, at 14.2–15.2, are a hand higher again.

The Fell pony breeders were delighted to see Prince Philip competing at Lowther with a team of their ponies, which they regarded as a great compliment to the breed. The new team did very well and can only serve as very valuable publicity for a society which has a huge membership of nearly a thousand. All their shows are very well supported and more and more breeders are finding that the demand for their ponies exceeds the supply.

With a milking herd requiring a considerable amount of attention, the Bells try to confine their showing to local fixtures within a radius of 40 miles, where they can avoid too early a start after milking, and return home at night.

THE DALES PONY

The Dales pony is a miniature cart-horse, inhabiting the upper dales of Tyne, Allen, Wear and Tees, which all descend from Killhope, the summit of which is 2,200ft above sea level. Killhope and the surrounding hills of Northumberland, Durham and North-west Yorkshire were once the centre of extensive lead-mining, and Dales ponies were used in great numbers to carry the lead ore on their backs from the mines in the hills to the washing places in the dales, and thence right into Newcastle upon Tyne. One miner could take charge of a team of some twenty ponies, which were caught wild off the hills, and each pony could carry a couple of hundredweight of ore in panniers, so that 2 tons of ore could be transported at one time, employing only one man for the journey.

These pack-ponies were the forerunners of the present Dales pony, although they have since been bred up to a standard height of 14.2–15.2hh by the thrifty dalesmen in order that they might be fit to do any sort of work on the hillside farms. They were great walkers and very fast trotters, and almost every Dales pony stud card boasts of trotting records – some 3 minutes to the mile, often with 12 stone on their backs. The present-day Dales are more powerful and cobby in build, and they have gained these characteristics at the expense of their free shoulder action. Thus they have deteriorated as riding ponies in the last 130 years, although they are still ridden shepherding sheep on the hills, and many of farmers hunt them regularly.

Many of the Dales ponies are jet black, and other prevailing colours are brown or bay, with an occasional grey but never a chestnut or an odd-coloured pony. They grow an abundance of fine hair on their heels, by which the dalesmen set great store, and they have very good, showy action and put their feet down straight, although they are inclined to 'go wide' behind. Their heads are neat and pony-like, with small ears and fine throats and jaws, and their necks, although inclined to shortness, are very strong. Shoulders tend to be straight, and too upright, but their backs, loins and quarters are all that can be desired. The ribs are well sprung and tails well set on. They have immense bone and the best of feet, legs and joints, and they are free from all hereditary unsoundness.

The Dales Pony Improvement Society holds its annual breed show each May at Barnard Castle. Mr J. W. Dalton, whose Snowhope Stud was renowned, showed champions at Islington before and between the wars, and Snowhope Beauty won 272 first prizes and championships. Snowhope Heather Belle, foaled in 1939, won 253 firsts and championships and was never beaten for the Lewis Priestman Challenge Cup at Durham County. Linnel Comet was another

Plate 58 Roy B. Charlton's Dales pony stallion, Linnel Comet

famous pony, owned by the late Mr Roy Charlton, who did so much for both Fell and Dales breeds. As well as winning at the Royal and the NPS, Comet took numerous War Office premiums in Lake District shows, and was by Daddy's Lad, a very fast trotting pony who was exported to the Argentine. He was by Comet II, a 14.3 hands very heavy cob who trotted a mile in 3 minutes, by the Welsh cob Comet, foaled in 1851 and a famous champion trotter. Linnel Comet was jet black and 14.1 hands, and his blood is in most of the best Dales ponies of the present day.

At the Royal Show in 1986, both championship and reserve were won by Mr J. W. Dickinson, who has a car-breaking business in Leeds but lives at Horsforth, north of the city, where he keeps three Dales mares and drives them in trade turnout classes. His hobby used to be riding motorbikes, but he considered himself too old for that sport and took up driving ponies instead in 1978. During the summer he shows regularly and thoroughly enjoys it. He won the championship with Acram Rose, a black mare by Heather Boy, and the reserve with May Queen, by the same sire.

THE HIGHLAND PONY

The largest and strongest of all the moorland breeds, the Highland pony, falls into two distinct categories – the pony of Barra and the Outer Isles, which is known as the Western Isle pony and ranges from 12.2 to 13.2 hands in height, and the bigger and stronger Mainland pony, who averages some 14.2 hands and is used by the crofters and smallholders, as well as for deerstalking, and makes nothing of carrying a 20-stone stag. Both types are immensely strong and well balanced, sure-footed and active over rough and boggy ground, and are of an extremely hardy and robust constitution. Although their home is the deer forest and the grouse moor, many have penetrated into England.

The Highland pony probably came originally from northern Asia, after the Ice Age in Europe, and in 1535 King James IV was presented by Louis XII of France with a choice selection of the best French breeds in order to increase the size of the ponies in the Scottish Highlands. Arab blood has since been used to produce a lighter type, and in other districts, where the ponies do the farm work, draught blood has been employed to produce additional substance. But the breed is sufficiently potent to have retained its chief characteristics, and today breeders are able to have recourse to different strains within the breed to obtain a versatile pony, all of which are ideal for hill work.

The colours most favoured are varying shades of dun and dark cream, with the characteristic black eel mark down the back and often zebra markings on the forelegs. Blacks, browns and bays are numerous, and many of the Mainland ponies are grey, and descend from the stallion Herd Laddie, who was foaled in Lochaber in 1881 and stood in Atholl for nearly thirty years. The coat consists of strong, badger-like top hairs over a fleecy undercoat.

Mr James Cairns started showing Highlands in 1912, when he began with the great grandam of his champion mare Calliach Bhan IX. The old mare was one of the famous Atholl Stud, and her foal Calliach Bhan III had an unbeaten record in the show-ring, including the championship of the Victory Royal Highland Show in 1919. This mare lived until she was 26 years old, producing 13 filly foals and 3 colts. Her great-great-granddaughter, a 14.1hh dun, foaled in 1944, was by Faillie Rover out of Calliach Bhan VIII. Reserve champion at the Royal Highland in 1949, she was also champion and reserve at Perth. Her dam was over 20 when she was born and could not feed

Plate 59 Three generations of Mr James Cairns' Highland ponies: Calliach Bhan III, Calliach Bhan IX and Calliach Bhan XI

Plate 60 Highland pony stallions (Leslie Lane)

her, so she was hand-reared on cow's milk. She is so placid and friendly that she failed to show herself at times.

Mr Donald Lamont of Invervack, Calvine, Perthshire, owned and bred the champion 14 hands grey-dun stallion Glengarry III. Foaled in 1947, by Monarch from June XIII by Boy David, he won at Perth at 2 and at 3 years was reserve champion. At the age of 5 he was champion at the NPS in London, winning the Princess Margaret and *Horse & Hound* cups and in 1953 was champion at both the NPS and Ponies of Britain (Ascot) shows, winning the Atholl Trophy, and first at the Royal. In 1954 and 1955 he was supreme champion at the Royal Highland.

The Department of Agriculture at Inverness (now, alas, disbanded) bred two of the best Highland ponies in recent years, Knock na Gael Marksman, whose head was so perfect that it was stuffed and hangs in the Edinburgh Dick Veterinary College and is also used as a logo for the Highland Pony Society. Equally outstanding was Glenrannoch, who in the 1960s made history by being the only stallion to win both in-hand and ridden championships at the Royal Highland Show. He stood at stud with Miss Georgie Henschel at Kincraig in Inverness, who was good enough to furnish these details and tells me that the modern Highland pony has been slimmed down and now that he is not shown so fat, people are beginning to realise that he can do a job of work as well as any other native breed of pony.

Her Majesty the Queen has also bred a Highland pony stallion, Balmoral Dee, who was shown successfully at the Royal Highland as a 3-year-old and is now 6. He stands at public stud near Balmoral, and three mares are kept at Balmoral.

159

THE · HACKNEY · HORSE

The origin of the Hackney, like that of any other old-established breed of horse, is largely a matter for conjecture, but it is reasonably certain that he is descended from Thoroughbreds on one side and from heavier breeds on the other. The most generally accepted theory is that the Darley Arabian, pillar of the General Stud Book, also left his mark to a substantial degree on the present-day Hackney, for in 1715 he sired the chestnut Flying Childers out of Betty Leedes, and Flying Childers was subsequently the sire of Blaze. The latter, foaled in 1733, afterwards travelled in Norfolk, which county gained a great reputation for the excellence of its Hackneys, or Norfolk trotters, which had been bred up in even earlier times by Eastern sires out of trotting and Flemish light draught mares.

Blaze was the sire of the first Shales (of which there were several), who was foaled in 1755, and also of Driver, foaled ten years later. Jenkinson's Fireaway (1780) and West's Fireaway (1800) were both by Driver, and from this line came the great Danegelt, who was foaled in 1879 and died at the age of 15, having enjoyed a remarkable career both in the show-ring and at stud. West's Fireaway sired Burgess's Fireaway (1815) and he was the sire of Wildfire, another great name in Hackney history. He was foaled in 1827, and eight years later his son Phenomenon was born. Phenomenon was the sire of Performer, grandsire of Sir Charles and great-grandsire of Denmark, sire of Danegelt.

Phenomenon was sold into Yorkshire as a 3-year-old, to be put to Yorkshire mares, and, standing for many years at Market Weighton with Mr Robert Ramsdale, improved the breed very much. Indeed, the Yorkshire Hackney is said to have become bigger and more powerful than its East Anglian counterpart in the course of time.

Old Shales, the fountain-head of many famous modern Hackney

strains, had a trotting record of 17 miles an hour, which was a very useful speed on the bad roads that prevailed at that time, and Phenomena, a 12-year-old 14.2 hands mare, trotted 4 miles in less than 11 minutes in 1800. These early Hackneys, whose task in life was to carry a burly farmer, and possibly his wife as well, to market, and to do odd jobs on the farm for the rest of the week, were, however, probably pretty coarse and stoutly built in comparison with the modern show Hackney, who requires both elegance and action. Thus it may be imagined that the Hackney, getting away from the old foundation stock, became finer bred as the years went by until he developed into the bloodlike king of the show-ring that we know today.

Denmark and Lord Derby II were probably the most famous of the Hackney sires, while Confidence was the most celebrated of the Norfolk breed. Denmark was a chestnut, 15.2hh, foaled in 1862 by Sir Charles out of Merryman, who won at the Great Yorkshire Show at the age of 23 with Denmark as a foal at foot. Denmark became an extremely fashionable sire, and his most famous son was Danegelt, for whom the late Sir Walter Gilbey gave 5,000 guineas, while his daughter Ophelia was said to be the greatest brood mare in the history of the breed. Denmark won many prizes in the show-ring, but his achievements at stud were even greater.

Lord Derby II, a dark-brown horse, was foaled in 1871, by Lord Derby out of Nancy, and his blood, especially when crossed with that of Denmark, has produced some of the most distinguished Hackneys, while he was equally successful in the show-ring. A third Yorkshire stallion, Triffett's Fireaway, deserves mention, especially as a sire of brood mares, among which was Jenny Bother'em, the dam of Ophelia.

In conformation, the good Hackney follows, in general, the lines of any other horse, and the shoulders are one of the most important points, for, unless they are long, they lack flexibility, and if they do not slope well backwards, they will not produce smoothness of action. The chest is broad and deep but depth of girth is not so apparent in the Hackney as it is, for instance, in the hunter, owing to the fact that he is also exceptionally deep about the back ribs, producing a comparatively level lower line.

The overall impression is of activity, strength and symmetry, plus great gaiety and elegance of carriage. The action is the most characteristic and the most important feature of the breed, and requires dash, fire and freedom of action, with smoothness and levelness of motion. No horse in existence is capable of extension to compare with that of a champion Hackney, and here it is the shoulders that do the greatest work, although the knees, pasterns, stifles and hocks are used in harmony with the shoulders to produce the incomparable and distinctive 'one-two-three-four'. Immense liberty in the shoulder action, therefore, is followed by the forelegs shooting forwards with bent knees and pasterns while, to ensure the important 'all round' action, the hind legs, with hocks and stifles well bent, provide propulsion. Crisp hock action is as important to the expert as is brilliant front action, and shoulder action is the most important of all, for without it a horse will fail to 'get away in front' by virtue of using his knees more strongly than his shoulders, and the result is a 'fighting' style of going, in which the animal lifts his knees up to his chin, to put his feet down again only inches away from the place whence he picked them up. Free, progressive action is the trademark of the genuine goer.

The most famous Hackney exhibitors, possibly of all time, are members of the Black family, whose establishment, owned by Messrs Robert and James Black, was originally at Osbaldwick, York, but moved south to Maiden Erlegh, Reading, in the 1930s. Some four or five years before World War II, James Black started his own establishment in stables adjacent to Solly Joel's old house, and since Robert Black's retirement the Maiden Erlegh Stud Farm was operated as a Thoroughbred stud by the Hon Mrs Beattie. His daughter Cynthia, who married Frank Haydon shortly before the war, established with her husband the most successful stable and stud in the country – first at Sleeches Farm, High Hurstwood, Uckfield, then at Shovelstrode Farm, near East Grinstead, then in the Cotswolds – first near Cirencester, then at Lower Slaughter, finally at Addlestrop. Frank Haydon first exhibited Hackneys in his early teens, driving for his father; Cynthia, who is at least the equal of the most brilliant of gentlemen whips, has been showing Hackneys since she was only slightly older, having commenced her career with a team of ponies belonging to the late Bertram Mills.

It would be invidious to single out any one owner of harness horses, were it not that for many years he was out on his own, both as breeder and exhibitor. Sir Nigel Colman owned twenty-one champions, many of them bred by himself. His family bred Hackneys in Norfolk for many years, and his father, the late F. E. Colman, of

Nork Park, Epsom Downs, was one of the earliest members of the Hackney Horse Society, founded in 1883 for the encouragement and improvement of the breed. Sir Nigel's mother, too, was an enthusiastic breeder and exhibitor, and on the death of her husband she carried on the stud from 1900, which her son duly inherited. Thus Sir Nigel had a lifelong experience of the harness horse, not only as owner but also as whip and judge.

He showed his first Olympia champion, Authority, in 1908, and in the same year he bought the 4-year-old Polonius mare Christolia as wheeler to him. In 1917 he sent her to the champion sire Mathias A I, and she foaled a superbly moving brown filly, Silhouette of Nork, who became a great winner and later a great brood mare. At the Doncaster Hackney Show in 1929 he bought the supreme champion mare, a 3-year-old called Modern Maid, by Mersey Searchlight out of Flash Clara by Royal Danegelt, and she was never beaten in-hand, winning the National Hackney Show female championship again in 1938.

Modern Maid was sent soon after her purchase to Bob and James Black, who were still at York, to be produced in harness, and in 1930 she came out as a 4-year-old to sweep the board, winning the supreme championship of the first joint show of the Royal Counties and HHS at Reading with consummate ease. For the next three years she was champion at both the National Hackney and International Horse Shows, but in 1934 she was beaten at Olympia by Mrs Henriques' brilliant stallion, Fleetwood Viking. These two great champions battled it out again in each of the two successive years, the stallion finally triumphing on both occasions.

Among the animals that Sir Nigel inherited from his mother was the mare Crystal of Nork, and in 1930 he put her to Mersey Searchlight, thus acquiring Nork Spotlight, who was destined to become a sire of immortal fame as well as a brilliant show horse. Spotlight won the junior championship and was reserve supreme champion at the NHS as a 2-year-old, and repeated the performance the following year, when the champion was his own father. He came out in harness in 1935, and was only once beaten in novice classes that year. Already, young as he was, he was making a name as a sire too, for in 1933 Bob Black sent him his good mare Allerthorpe Carnation. The filly foal from this mating was the great brood mare Erlegh Maiden, who won the yearling class and junior championship at the NHS in 1935, when her sire was still only a 4-year-old.

Spotlight was also used by Mr Albert Throup, who bred from him the sires Warwick Footlight and Warwick Pegasus, which line eventually produced Mr W. T. Barton's champion, Walton Diplomat. It was indeed fortunate for posterity that breeders used Spotlight as early as they did, for he died when he was only 8 years old. His first major win was at the NHS in 1936, where he was supreme champion, beating Fleetwood Viking after an epic duel. In 1937 their positions were reversed, but the following year Spotlight beat Viking at the NHS, although beaten by him at Richmond and Olympia.

In 1934 Spotlight was put to his owner's mare, Silhouette of Nork, and the resulting colt foal was said to be the best of Sir Nigel's many champions, Nork Monoplane. He won as a stallion in-hand as a yearling at the NHS, as a 2-year-old was junior and reserve supreme champion, junior and supreme champion at 3 and supreme again in 1939. In harness, he was novice champion in 1938 at the NHS, where his sire was supreme champion, and supreme at Olympia. The next year he was supreme at the NHS, and it was then unique for the same horse to win both led and driven championships at this show – although since then his full brother, Black Magic of Nork, has repeated this double.

In 1939 Monoplane's dam foaled a full brother to him, Black Magic. Owing to the war, he could not be shown until 1946, when he created a sensation at the NHS at Crewe, and won the supreme championship harness award. He was broken and always driven in the show-ring (other than in amateur classes) by James Black, who had driven the supreme champion at the International Horse Show no fewer than 14 times – a wonderful record. Sir Nigel won the Hackney supreme championship 9 times out of 12 National Hackney Shows from 1930 to 1947.

Magic's numerous successes in the show-ring include supreme championships at the International, the NHS, Richmond, Windsor and the Royal, and no stallion in the history of the breed has rivalled him, in that his successes were both in-hand and in harness and include winning the IHS supreme championship no fewer than six times. In 1956, in-hand, he won the NHS supreme championship, and the special prize for the best horse in the show, for the seventh time, and at the 1955 show his 3-year-old daughter, Nork Quicksilver, bred by Sir Nigel, won the supreme championship for mares. This was the first occasion in the history of the show – first held in 1885 – that any exhibitor won both in-hand championships with home-bred animals. In harness, Magic won the supreme championship for two successive years, 1946–7.

It is significant that all but one of the remaining post-war champions have been either bred or produced, or both, by Mr and Mrs Frank Haydon, who also owned the triple champion stallion, Solitude, and that immortal brood mare, Erlegh Maiden – bred, as mentioned earlier, by Mr Bob Black.

Solitude, a bay horse, 15.1hh was foaled in 1933 and bred by Joseph Morton at Downham Market, Norfolk, by Buckley Courage out of Dark Vision. He was never shown in harness, owing to the war, and, like Magic, was first shown in 1946 at the NHS at Crewe, winning his class, the senior stallion championship, was supreme champion stallion and supreme champion animal of the show – which honours he achieved again in 1947 and 1948, after which he was retired from the ring. The better part of his showing years were lost, for he was 13 years old in 1946 and his owners considered his value to the breed as a stud horse was far too great to warrant a

Plate 61 Mr Frank Haydon's great Hackney stallion, Solitude

continuation of his show career. How right was their decision may be gauged by the fact that Solitude's sons and daughters have won him a worldwide reputation. He is represented by his progeny in the USA, Australia, Canada, Holland, Portugal, South Africa and South America, while his offspring won the supreme harness championship at the NHS at six out of ten post-war meetings, while he sired the winning produce group for eight years running, 1947–53, and again in 1956. In 1955 his grandchildren, by Hurstwood Commander, won the produce group.

Solitude was a magnificent horse of great character and nearly perfect conformation, and an outstandingly good temperament. He was bought from Mr Avery in 1945, the 'dead image' of his illustrious sire '. . . brimful of quality, with a practically perfect outline, well ribbed up and a brilliant all-round mover who thrilled everyone privileged to see him.'

There has been no mare since Ophelia in the history of the breed to equal Erlegh Maiden, who was foaled in 1934 and died twenty years later. A 15-hand bay, she was first shown at the NHS as a yearling, where she won her class, the junior championship and was reserve supreme champion female, after which she became the property of Mrs McColl. She won her class again in 1936 and was not only junior champion but supreme female champion as well. As a 3-year-old she staged a repeat performance, and as a 4-year-old in 1938 she was champion in-hand, reserve champion novice harness horse at the NHS and champion novice at Olympia. The following year she won again at the NHS and earned many championships in harness at subsequent leading shows.

Early in 1944, Frank Haydon purchased her, through his father-in-law who bred her, from the executors of the late Mr R. H. McColl, and later that year she foaled Hurstwood Supremo, by Solitude. Supremo, who was exported to the United States in 1950, was junior champion stallion and reserve supreme animal (to his sire) at the NHS. In 1948 he was supreme champion novice.

In 1945, Erlegh Maiden foaled Hurstwood Commander, also by Solitude. This horse was seldom shown in harness, having received an injury as a foal, but he was used for stud and his progeny won him second place in the produce group at the NHS in 1954 and first in 1955. His first foal, Hurstwood Creation, exported to Australia, won numerous prizes at the Sydney Royal Show.

Erlegh Maiden's 1946 foal was Hurstwood Lonely Lady, also by

Solitude, sold to Mrs B. H. Mellor. She was junior champion and supreme female champion at the NHS in both 1947 and 1948, which accomplishment on the part of a yearling and a 2-year-old created a record in the history of the breed. In 1953 she was Harness Horse of the Year at Harringay and in 1954 she was the supreme champion harness horse at the NHS, driven by Dick Midgley. In 1956 she was the champion mare at the breed show at Derby for the third time, another record.

In 1947 Erlegh Maiden foaled Hurstwood Lonely Maid by Solitude, and she was first and reserve junior champion to her sister in 1948, and beat Lonely Lady for the supreme female championship in 1949. Supreme champion amateur-driven animal in 1954 for her owner, Mrs Mellor, she was then exported to Canada.

The fifth foal by Solitude from Erlegh Maiden was their second (1955) supreme champion harness horse, Hurstwood Superlative, a bay mare, 15.1¼ hands and foaled in 1948. Exceptionally temperamental and highly strung, Superlative was not shown until 1953, when Mrs Haydon produced her in harness at Windsor, where she won the supreme championship. That season she was champion novice harness horse and was never beaten, her successes including Richmond, the IHS, the NHS and the Royal. In 1954 she was supreme champion at the Royal and beat every top animal she met bar Black Magic, to whom she was reserve supreme at the IHS, beating her two illustrious sisters. By 1955 she was recognised as one of the greatest actioned harness horses the breed has ever known, and she became the season's supreme champion, driven by Mrs Haydon for Captain R. S. de Q. Quincey of Marden, Herefordshire, who was also a great expert on cattle as well as an avid gardener and grower of exotic flowers. In 1956 she was again supreme. Prior to her début in harness she produced a son, Hurstwood Consul, who was junior champion at the NHS in 1953 and 1954, and in 1955, as a 4-year-old, supreme champion novice harness horse – another record achievement.

In 1949 and 1950 Erlegh Maiden had the misfortune to have dead foals, but in 1951 she foaled Hurstwood Demoiselle by Walton Diplomat, and this filly was first, junior champion and supreme champion female at the NHS in both 1953 and 1954. Her 1952 foal by Hurstwood Commander, Hurstwood Dictator, was not shown as a youngster, but her last, Hurstwood Donazella (by Walton Diplomat), won at the NHS as a yearling and 2-year-old.

It is probable that in years to come Erlegh Maiden will be proved to have had as much effect upon the breed as did Ophelia, to whom nearly every top animal traces back, mainly through her sons Matthias and Polonius, and her daughter Grace – none of which were great individuals in themselves. Thus, Erlegh Maiden may even surpass Ophelia, for not only have her offspring proved themselves good breeders, but they have themselves been champion harness animals.

Mr W. T. Barton of Redhill, whose horses were also produced from High Hurstwood, had the enviable distinction of possessing the harness mare who was acclaimed repeatedly as the animal of the century – the incomparable Holywell Florette, supreme champion harness horse for four seasons, from 1949 until she retired in 1952. A liver chestnut, 14.3½hh, foaled in 1943, she was bred by that great enthusiast Claude Goddard, by Solitude out of Lavington Flavia.

Mr Goddard, a past president of the Hackney Horse Society, died in 1945, and among those attending his dispersal sale was Billy Barton, whose intention it was to bid for a pony coach. The coach in question was evidently in demand, for it went for 750 guineas and was bought in, so Mr Barton, chagrined at his loss, made his way to the horse-ring. He had not intended to buy any horses, but he noticed a well-known breeder bidding for a washy-looking chestnut filly and the insidious appeal of an auction became too much for him. He matched the breeder's 270-guinea bid with one of 300, and thus he acquired Florette. Away from the lure of the sale-ring, he was assailed by doubts as to the wisdom of his purchase, which were mollified only slightly when he read in the press that the bargain of the Goddard sale was the filly acquired by W. T. Barton – the opinion of that prescient judge of the breed, the late Geoffrey Bennett.

Florette, sent to High Hurstwood to be broken and produced, continued to hide her light for some time, but gradually her washy colour deepened to rich liver chestnut and she grew and furnished, while her carriage and action developed accordingly. As a 3-year-old she was already beginning to reveal her potentialities, and the following year they became even more apparent. She came out in 1947, and with her snowy-white stockings and blaze she attracted much attention, but she was still not quite ready or mature and she had only five outings that season.

In 1948 Florette commenced her great career, which was destined to make that of any Hackney that had been shown for the previous fifty years pale into comparative insignificance. She won the supreme championship at Windsor, and she ultimately won this award at the first of the big London shows five times in succession. Five times did she stand supreme at Blackpool, too, and she scored a quartet of successes at the NHS, Richmond and the Royal, and was three times champion at the International – the scene of her only defeat at the height of her career. For one year she refused to settle and was beaten in her class by Black Magic – although two days later the judges reversed their decision and awarded her the championship.

Florette's great liberty and scope of action, her rhythm, pace and power that were wholly unique, would have enabled her to go on winning with Cynthia Haydon at the other end of the ribbons for an indefinite period, but by the time she was 9 she had trebled and quadrupled every supreme award that lay open to her, and her most logical destination was to become a brood mare – particularly as her brother, Dufferin Haven, was the supreme champion stallion of the USA and Canada in 1952. She was therefore retired, and although she produced a dead foal to Walton Diplomat in 1953, the following September she had a chestnut filly with four white legs to Craigwell Lochinvar which paraded with its mother at Harringay as a yearling.

Mr Barton had another supreme champion harness horse to follow in Florette's footsteps in 1953 – Walton Diplomat, a bay stallion, 14.3½ hands, bred at Warrington by Mr A. Green, by Fairbrother Spotlight out of Walton Beauty. A horse of great character, tremendous courage and beautiful conformation, he was first produced in harness by Mrs Haydon at Windsor in 1951 as a 4-year-old. He disgraced himself in the ring, being a young stallion of exceptional courage, and as he had travelled badly in the horse-box he refused to settle and was put second to Hurstwood Lonely Lady. At Richmond, however, he was champion novice and also at the NHS, remaining unbeaten in novice classes for the rest of the season.

After the débâcle at Windsor, several well-wishers of some notability advised both his owner and the Haydons to geld Diplomat, maintaining that it would never be safe to show him in harness as an entire. Happily, they all decided to persevere, and in 1953 he was supreme champion harness horse, having beaten all the top horses with the exception of his stable companion Hurstwood Superlative, against whom he never competed. As a sire, although still comparatively young, he was responsible for the winning produce group in

1954, the junior champion stallion in 1953 and 1954, the junior female champion in 1953, the junior and supreme champion female in 1954 and the supreme champion novice harness horse (Hurstwood Consul, then thought to be the sire of the future) in 1955.

During the last thirty years the most outstanding horses have been:

Hurstwood Superlative (1956–9).
Outwood Florescent (1967–73) – the only Hackney to have been harness champion for seven years in succession. A son of Holywell Florette (harness champion 1949–52) by Solitude.
Brook Acres Light Mist (1974–7) by Walton Searchlight (Supreme Champion Stallion 1958–60) out of a Solitude mare.
Hurstwood Director (1980 and 1981) by Walton Searchlight out of a Walton Diplomat mare. Owned by Mrs J. A. McDougald of Canada, a great supporter of the breed who also owns a four-in-hand team which competed regularly in the FEI driving events (based on the ridden three-day event). Director did not compete in 1983 as he was involved in the Centenary Display at the National Hackney Show. He died in 1984 but left four progeny, one of whom, Hurstwood Gondolier, was junior and reserve supreme at the NHS in 1986.

The three owners who have dominated the scene have been the late Captain R. S. de Q. Quincey, who owned Hurstwood Superlative and the 1962 and 1964 champion Marden Midas; the late Mrs D. S. Hughes and her son Michael, the owners of Craigweil Maybole and Outwood Florescent; and the late Kenneth G. Moss with Brook Acres Light Mist. Other champions were:

Craigweil Maybole, 1960, 1961, 1965 and 1966, also Supreme Champion Hackney Stallion 1962 and 1964 and from 1967 to 1970.
Sherwood Forest Queen, 1963, by Hurstwood Consul, a son of Hurstwood Superlative by the 1953 champion Walton Diplomat, owned by Miss Scrivener.
Holypark What's Wanted, also by Hurstwood Consul, 1978 for Dutch exhibitor T. C. Middelman and 1984 for Mr and Mrs B. Turner.
Brookfield Harvest Moon, 1979, by a son of Solitude and out of a daughter of Holywell Florette, exhibited by Mrs E. and Miss P. Peters.
Holypark Rantara, 1982–3, by Holypark What's Wanted, owned by Mr J. Wenham.
Whitehavens Step High, 1985–6, by Suddie Sovereign, who traces back to Solitude and Erlegh Maiden, owned by Mrs E. E. Vyse.

All these champions are linked, as will be seen, to the Hurstwood Stud, being either bred at the stud or exhibited from the stud or descendants from Hurstwood Stud bloodlines. Mrs Haydon drove the Harness champions on twenty-three occasions and she drove the

Hackney Pony champions on twenty-five occasions – two incredible, surely never-to-be equalled records. When she and Frank really retire it will be the end of an era that will never be repeated.

I shall never forget the European Driving Championships in Zug, Switzerland, which I was covering for *The Times* in 1981. Horses and their attendants from many nations on either side of the Iron Curtain were assembled in the stable area, the British camp led by Prince Philip with the Queen's team of Cleveland Bays. There was a marvellous atmosphere of camaraderie and Frank and Cynthia Haydon, with their popular German secretary Annie, who has been with them for twenty years and acquired a Yorkshire accent in the process, held open house in the canvas extension to their caravan where cups of delicious tea, good company and lots of entertaining chat were a godsend on a hot, muggy afternoon. What fun it all was, and how much the Haydons contributed to it!

THE HACKNEY PONY

The Hackney pony was evolved by the late Mr Christopher Wilson of Kirkby Lonsdale, Westmorland, a keen 'pony' man whose ambition was to breed a pocket edition of the Hackney horse, combining pony characteristics with the good looks and superlative action of his larger brother. How well he succeeded may be judged by the present-day champions. There was a time, shortly after World War I, when the average Hackney pony had degenerated into a whippety creature with a diminutive body, bred solely for action, and although there are still a few of these to be seen today, the best Hackney ponies are not, we are told, dissimilar to their prototypes – butty little fellows, whose conformation and middlepiece leave nothing to be desired.

Mr Wilson's strain of ponies was initiated by the use of a small Hackney stallion, Sir George, upon native Fell pony mares. Sir George was foaled, in 1866, by the 15.2hh Hart's Sportsman (pure Yorkshire Hackney blood) out of a mare called Polly. He won at eight consecutive Royal shows and proved to be an extremely potent sire. Mr Wilson mated the Fell cross fillies back to their sire, and often even staged a repeat performance in the succeeding generation, so that the Wilson ponies sometimes carried three crosses of Sir George's blood, and this policy had astoundingly successful results. He also purchased a Thoroughbred mare called The Pet, and won with her twice at the Royal. The Pet produced the 13.3hh mare Snorer, and she won at the Royal for five years in succession, won the Queen's Gold Medal and the Hackney Horse Society's prize at Windsor's Jubilee Show in 1887, and was champion at the London Hackney Show in 1893–4.

In 1882, Mr Wilson mated Snorer with the 13.2 hands stallion Young Confidence (by the famous Hackney sire D'Oyley's Confidence out of a Welsh pony mare) who had won at three Royal shows. The colt foal, who was registered as Little Wonder II, sired Sir Horace, the greatest pony sire of all time; and a later filly, Dorothy Derby II, was the dam of another famous pony, Julius Caesar II.

Mr Wilson sold his stud in 1892, and a number of ponies went to Sir Humphrey de Trafford, who, three years later, sold on five mares at an average price of over 700 guineas a head, the 3-year-old filly, Miss Sniff, who was the most inbred of them all, making a top price of 900 guineas. The best ponies, however, including Sir Horace and his sister, eventually came into the possession of Sir Gilbert Greenall (later the first Lord Daresbury), who founded the most successful stud of all time at Tissington, Derbyshire.

Other very successful studs of Hackney ponies have had a far-reaching effect on the breed at later dates, one being the strain founded by the late David Sowerby, MRCVS, at Hull. He bought a 13.1 hands mare called Polly by the 15.2 hands stallion Trifitt's Fireaway, and put her to the stallions Denmark and Lord Derby II. The colt by the former was Sir Gibbie, and Polly's daughter by the latter was Lady Ethel. Both ponies, well under 13 hands, were bought by Sir Gilbert Greenall after the Sowerby strain had been developed, and at the annual Tissington sales Mr J. E. Kerr of Harviestoun Castle (and of Shetland pony fame) bought as many of the family as he could. At the Tissington dispersal sale many of the best of Polly's family went to Sussex, and to Mrs A. C. King of Braishfield, who acquired the Sir Gibbie stallion Tissington Gideon and six mares tracing back to Polly, and founded a stud which, with the Harviestoun Stud, is one of the most famous of recent times.

The late Alfred S. Day of Crewe founded another noted stud in 1892, with stock bought from Norfolk – primarily, the 13.3 hands brown stallion Berkeley Model, and his mother, brothers and sister. Model became champion at the 1894 Hackney Show, and won again the following year, beating Sir Horace. He then became a great sire, and when he died his owner bought the London champion Fireboy, who was equally successful at stud. He was by Julius Caesar II out of the Norfolk-bred Cassius, by Lord Derby II.

Mr Day's Berkeley ponies were the foundation stock of both the Melbourne Stud in Yorkshire and the Talke Stud in Staffordshire, and also of the Shirbeck Stud in Lincolnshire which produced the great pony Billet Doux and the American champion, Highland Cora.

Next to Sir Horace, the most outstanding Hackney pony was the little brown Southwell Swell, who stood at Warrington until he was sold to the United States at the age of 13. He was by Sir Horace's sire, Pindersfield's Horace, out of a Berkeley Model mare, and his son Talke Bonfire sired Fireflash, father of the 1946–8 champion pony, Harlock Chiquita. The sire of many subsequent winners, Southworth Noni, goes back to Sir Horace in the male line and is out of a Southwell Swell mare.

Three ponies dominated the Hackney pony scene after World War II – Harlock Chiquita, Bossy and Oakwell Sir James. The first-named, a brown 12 hands mare, was foaled in 1936, out of Braishfield Chic, and was bred at Wetherby by J. W. Hemingway. She was first produced in the ring by Mrs Haydon in 1946, in the ownership of Mr Tom Neal, and early the following year she was bought by Frank Haydon and sold to Mrs B. H. Mellor. Chiquita was champion pony for the three seasons she was shown, 1946–8, and was never beaten as a pony in the whole of her show career, after which she was retired to stud.

Plate 62 Oakwell St James

Bossy was probably one of the most famous Hackney ponies, for his great character, personality and presence made him a great favourite with the crowds. Only 11.2 hands, he was a dark-brown pony, foaled in 1940, by Little Chief out of Ascot Belle, and he was bred at Broadlands, Ascot, by Frank C. Minoprio. He was first produced in 1948 for his then owner, Mrs Barbara Harcourt Wood, by Stanley Hinder, winning several novice classes and standing novice champion at the National Hackney Show, without making much headway in open classes. In 1949 Mrs Harcourt Wood sent him to the Haydons to be shown and Mrs Haydon brought him out at Richmond, where he was supreme champion harness pony. His owner won the supreme hack championship with Liberty Light and the supreme hunter championship with Ballykeane that same year at Richmond, surely an achievement which has never been equalled.

Bossy was virtually unbeaten for the rest of that season, and gained the supreme championship at the NHS. Later he was sold to Mr T. Wood Jones and he reigned supreme for the next two years, shown by Mr James Black. In 1951 he was bought by Mr and Mrs G. C. Kimpton, for whom he won the Harringay title. In 1952 he won at Richmond, the Royal and the IHS, but at the NHS and at Windsor he was beaten for the supreme award by Hurstwood Autocrat, shown by Mrs Haydon for Mr Campbell of the United States. In 1953 he won at Richmond and Windsor, but at the NHS, IHS and the Royal stood down to Oaklands Parader, also shown by Mrs Haydon and eventually sold to the USA. In 1954 at the NHS he was finally vanquished by Oakwell Sir James, of whom more anon, driven by Cynthia Haydon, who drove the champion pony at eight of the first ten postwar shows.

Bossy had some thousand prizes to his credit, and loved the applause he invariably attracted from the crowds. An extremely hot pony, he was nevertheless a wonderful traveller and always travelled loose in the horse-box with his pal, Waterdells Personality.

Oakwell Sir James, bred by the late G. A. Shepherd, was champion pony in-hand at the Hackney Breed Show from 1952 to 1956 and champion harness pony simultaneously from 1950. A brown stallion, 12.1½hh, he was foaled in 1946 by Broompark Sir John out of Carlestoun Summer's Dream. He was first produced in harness by Mrs Haydon in 1950 for Miss M. P. James, for whom he was champion novice pony at the NHS. In 1951 and 1952 he was shown from his owner's stable with moderate success, and in 1953 he

Plate 63 Highstone Nicholas

returned to High Hurstwood and his original driver and went through the season unvanquished, winning 9 firsts and 6 championships, among them the Harringay title. In 1954 he was supreme champion harness pony at the NHS and won 17 firsts and 12 championships. Soon after the end of that season he was bought by Frank Haydon, who sold him again during 1955 to the Hon Mrs Ionides. In 1955, Sir James was once again practically unbeaten, among his triumphs being the championships at Richmond, Windsor, the supreme pony championship at the NHS and the Hackney Pony of the Year title at Harringay. Again in 1956, no pony was a match for him and he retained his unbeaten status.

The Hackney pony scene was dominated by Highstone Nicholas (1957–62), owned by the late Hon Mrs N. Ionides, and his progeny – his sons Marden Finality, Marden Little Nick, Fairmile Gemini, Sunbeam Super Star and Hurstwood Consort, his grandson Marden Little Swell and his great-grandson, Hurstwood Untouchable.

Marden Finality, 1963, 1966, 1971–4 also champion pony stallion 1965 and 1967–75. Bred by the late Captain de Q. Quincey at the Hurstwood Stud and after his death purchased by Miss Robina S. Davidson.
Marden Little Nick, 1964–5, owned by the late Mrs A. Battine.
Fairmile Gemini, 1979, owned by Mr E. A. Ward.
Sunbeam Super Star, 1986, owned by Mrs E. E. Vyse.
Hurstwood Consort, champion pony stallion, 1976–84 (not shown in 1985 owing to Mrs Haydon's knee operation) and again in 1986. Also a

175

big winner in harness at the Royal International Horse Show and the Horse of the Year Show, being unbeaten at both. He has now retired to stud.

Marden Little Swell (by Marden Little Nick), 1970, 1976–7, owned by the late Mr K. G. Moss.

Hurstwood Untouchable (by Marden Little Swell), 1980–4, owned by the late Miss R. S. Davidson.

Sunbeam Lucky, 1985, owned by Mr and Mrs Vardy, traces back through his dam to Highstone Nicholas.

Vulcan Sir Richard, champion 1967–9, was by Oakwell Sir James. With the exception of Heathfield George, champion in 1975 and 1978, owned by Mr C. R. Cowan, again all the champions go back to Hurstwood Stud bloodlines, in particular Highstone Nicholas and Oakwell Sir James. Mrs Haydon drove the champions on twenty-five occasions.

The two most prominent owners during the last thirty years were the Hon Mrs Ionides and the late Miss R. S. Davidson, who is succeeded by her sister, Miss S. S. Davidson, as the owner of Hurstwood Untouchable and Hurstwood Consort. Although Mr and Mrs Haydon have not retired completely from the show-ring, they are only exhibiting at two or three major shows such as Royal Windsor, the National Hackney Show and the Royal International Horse Show. The NHS is held in conjunction with the South of England Show at Ardingly in Sussex.

Plate 64 Hurstwood Untouchable

The society's president for 1986, Mrs Haydon, said at the twenty-eighth annual dinner that she and Frank would be reducing their commitments after fifty years of producing, breeding and showing, and that she looks forward to seeing the younger generation flying the flag. Mr Christopher Hall, Chairman of the South of England Agricultural Association, thanked Mrs Haydon 'for her brilliant displays and for all the fun she has given' – for which I can vouch, having spent many happy hours in the Haydon caravan, which is always bursting at the seams, after the shows at the White City, Wembley, Harringay, Ardingly, and on one memorable occasion at Belle Vue, Manchester (a misnomer, if ever there was one) when, after a somewhat alcoholic prelude, we all repaired to the fun fair, and hazardous rides in the rain on a scenic railway and similar horrors, in 1956.

During non-Hackney times at the London shows, Cynthia Haydon sits in their caravan and embroiders tapestry to relax. On one occasion she was driving home from White City to Sussex when she saw one of the ponies who had been competing in the coster class labouring ahead of her along the road. He was patently not a prize-winner; his ribs were nearly protruding through his coat, he was desperately tired and pathetically old. She pulled up and asked the pony's driver how much he would take for the animal. He named his price, she offered hers. He took it with alacrity. The decrepit old pony was driven down to Shovelstrode Farm and unboxed, an incongruous addition to all those immaculate Hackneys.

Domiciled in Shepherd's Bush, he grazed ravenously as soon as he was turned out, probably not having seen grass for years. Sadly, they soon noticed that he was 'quidding' – leaving a trail of grass behind him as the gaps between his teeth allowed it to escape. But he had enjoyed life tremendously until the veterinary surgeon agreed that it would be kinder to put him down.

How many exhibitors – and professionals, at that – would have responded, as Mrs Haydon did, to the sight of that old pony? It is so much easier to 'pass by on the other side'.

Mrs Haydon drove all the champion horses except Sherwood Forest Queen, Holypark What's Wanted, Brookfield Harvest Moon, Holypark Rantara and Whitehavens Step High; in ponies, all except Fairmile Gemini, Sunbeam Super Star, Sunbeam Lucky and Heathfield George.

THE · INTERNATIONAL CHAMPIONS

It is always especially thrilling when a home-bred champion emerges in the field of international endeavour, and no one horse gave us more to cheer about than Brigadier Michael Gordon-Watson's Cornishman V. Ridden by his owner's daughter, Mary, he won the European Individual Championship at Haras du Pin in Normandy in 1969. A year later, at Punchestown in Co Kildare, Ireland, he won the World Championship for Britain over a course concerning which the least said, the better. Suffice it to add that when I asked Mary which, if any, fence she enjoyed jumping, she replied without hesitation: 'The last – simply because it *was* the last!'

'Corny' was by Golden Surprise, an HIS premium stallion who ran with his mares, out of a mare called Polly IV and had won several point-to-points, although not in the General Stud Book. She was inclined to be slightly scatty, as were her progeny, not excluding her most illustrious son in his youth. When the brigadier left his home near Cranborne in Dorset to try the newly broken youngster in Cornwall, he was bucked off into the midden. Nothing daunted, he bought him. Foaled in 1959, Corny was then 4 years old. Five years later, he won his first of two team gold medals for Britain in Mexico, 1968, ridden not by Mary but by Richard Meade.

Mary would not have been selected for the British Olympic team in any case, being too young and inexperienced at that time. But she rode Corny at the Royal International that year at Wembley in the working hunter class when she fell off him and broke her leg, putting herself out of action. The horse, however, was needed for the Olympic effort, so he was offered and accepted with alacrity. The Gordon-Watsons hoped that he would be ridden by Sergeant Ben Jones of the King's Troop, RHA, when Mrs A. B. Whiteley's Foxdor, his usual mount, died suddenly, because he instructed at their Pony Club camp every year and knew Cornishman well. But Captain Martin Whiteley, who had broken his back riding a race in Germany,

Plate 65 Mary Gordon-Watson and Cornishman V (who hated presentations, as his ears might indicate!) receiving their World Championship Trophy from Captain Harry Freeman-Jackson at Punchestown in 1970

offered Sgt Jones the ride on his good horse, The Poacher, so Cornishman was given by the selectors to Richard Meade, for whom he went very well.

It had been Ben Jones who had put Mary and Cornishman together – she had started riding and hunting the 17-hand bay when she was 11 – and they were always a partnership with enormous rapport. They hunted locally with the Portman, the Blackmore Vale and the Wilton, and then they used to set off for Leicestershire on Sundays, hunt with the Quorn on Mondays and return home on Tuesdays. 'Just think what that would cost nowadays!' adds Thalia Gordon-Watson, Mary's mother.

Two years after they won the world title, Mary and Corny were selected for the British team to defend their gold medals in the Olympic Games in Munich. With Richard Meade on Major Derek Allhusen's home-bred Laurieston, Captain Mark Phillips on Great

Ovation and Bridget Parker on Cornish Gold, they successfully defended their Olympic title. After the presentations by Prince Philip, Corny pulled like a train as the team galloped around the arena at Riem in their lap of honour, and Mary remarked afterwards that it was the most fraught moment for her of all the four days of the competition.

Corny rested on his laurels after that as far as the big-time was concerned, but competed in Spillers and such types of events for amusement (he was now 14) and naturally went on hunting – continuing, in fact, with gusto until March 1986, by which time he had reached the ripe old age of 27. Then he contracted a particularly painful form of laminitis, and it was deemed kindest to put him down rather than have him suffer. He had had a lovely life, given immense pleasure and happiness to his owners and his fans, who were legion, had acted in a film, which he thoroughly enjoyed, adored his hunting, and had the devoted Julie Baxter, who was trained at Bathampton by Lady Hugh Russell, to minister to his every need from 1970 for the rest of his life.

DAVID BROOME'S CHAMPIONS

David Broome, the most outstanding natural British show-jumping rider of the post-war era, has had some brilliant horses through his hands since he emerged at the top of the tree nationally at the age of 19 in 1959. He won an Olympic bronze medal in Rome in 1960 on Oliver Anderson's Sunsalve (by the premium stallion Skoiter), whom he recalls as the most fantastic Olympic performer he ever rode.

'He could do the most remarkable things,' he said. 'He was a natural.'

David's first good horse was Wildfire, a horse his father bought for £75 when he was drafted from the King's Troop, RHA, for consistent insubordination. When David was 19, he and Wildfire were the leading money winners of the year. Two years later David topped the list again, this time with Discutido, the former Argentine Olympic horse, who stopped with everyone else. David also won many prizes on Ballan Silver Knight and Bess, his sister's mare, and had to borrow Jacopo from his future brother-in-law, Ted Edgar, to ride in the Tokyo Olympics in 1964.

The following year, when he took over John Massarella's Irish-bred Mister Softee, his fortunes changed dramatically. In 1966 they

Plate 66 David Broome on Mister Softee at Hickstead in 1966 (Pony/Light Horse)

won the King George V Gold Cup, and, in addition to two more European titles in Rotterdam and at Hickstead (totalling three with the one he annexed on Sunsalve in Aachen in 1961), he also won the British Jumping Derby.

After winning his third European title, David said to me when I congratulated him: 'I hope everyone realises just what a brilliant horse he is and how privileged they are to see him. There isn't another like him anywhere.' He also won an Olympic bronze medal in Mexico City in 1968.

In 1970, David won the World Championship in La Baule, France, his mount being Douglas Bunn's Irish-bred Beethoven, by Roi d'Egypte, when his brilliant riding of Graziano Mancinelli's head-strong German horse, Fidux, was a major contributory factor to his victory.

In Munich in 1972, David rode in his fourth and last Olympic Games and then abandoned his amateur status, riding for Esso. Unfortunately, the oil crisis in the Middle East put paid to the renewal of the contract in 1974. In 1975 Phil Harris (now Sir Phil of Harris Carpets) commenced his sponsorship of David Broome and bought the 'elegant Yank', as David calls him, Philco. At the Horse of the Year Show, David won no fewer than seven competitions with the American horse, Sportsman (Irish-bred, by Chou Chin Chow) and Heatwave. On Heatwave, moreover, a newcomer to the Nations' Cup, he jumped the crucial round to give Britain victory in both the Prince of Wales Cup at Hickstead and the Aga Khan Trophy in Dublin.

In 1976 David won many events abroad and on Sportsman won the Champion Horseman and the *Daily Mail* Cup. In 1977 he was Britain's top rider, in 1978 he was in the team to win the World Championship in Aachen and again the leading rider at the Royal International, while Heatwave won the Irish Horse Board's special award as the leading international horse bred in Ireland. In 1979 he helped to win the European Championship in Rotterdam on Queensway Big Q and won Dublin's Irish Grand Prix on Sportsman, as well as assisting in the British Nations' Cup victories in Paris, Hickstead and Dublin. He also won the Netherlands Grand Prix on Big Q and the Amsterdam Grand Prix on Sportsman.

Bred in Derren, Mullagh, Co Clare, and sold to Mr Andrew Massarella as a 3-year-old at the Goffs sales at Ballsbridge, after he had been chased over a low pole by men flapping their mackintoshes, Mister Softee developed into 'a real work horse', David said. 'He was so sensitive that if he hit a fence he was really upset and cleared the next half-dozen by 6in or more.' When they were testing for signs of abuse to show-jumpers' legs at the Horse of the Year Show in 1966, they tested Softee three times and David was horrified that the authorities suspected him of getting at the horse, until he was reassured that for the good name of the sport they did not want the vets to catch anyone and were therefore only checking on the horses they knew were not abused.

David believes that Mister Softee was the best of his team – but little Sportsman (whom he refused ever to take to the Olympic Games because he was 'too good to risk') was his favourite. When the time came to retire him, unbeknown to David, he was taken from Wales up to Olympia for a public retirement ceremony – a highly emotive occasion for all concerned.

Thoroughbred stallions which are free of any hereditary disease or unsoundness and have passed the stringent veterinary examination required to certify a premium stallion on the Hunters' Improvement Society's register, are in constant demand in many countries. Last year six went abroad – to Portugal, Holland, West Germany, Italy, the United States and Canada (where there is a Canadian Hunters' Improvement Society). Bill Manning and Tub Ivens also sent horses to South Africa.

Cleveland Bay stallions and mares are used in the United States as foundation stock for hunter breeding, particularly in the southern states like Virginia, where they have been exported for many years. In fact, the Queen bought the outstandingly good Cleveland stallion, Mulgrave Supreme, in order to prevent him from being sent to the United States, and he did the breed a great deal of good. They are, of course, used in the state carriages and are always well represented in the Royal Mews, as well as being used in competitive driving by Prince Philip.

Hackney horses and ponies were exported last year to South Africa, the United States, Canada and Italy. Holland, the USA and Canada are regular customers of long standing. Italy, Australia and New Zealand, Germany, France and Sweden are frequent customers, and a new buyer in recent years has been Malta. Mrs Frank Haydon, who is the most famous and celebrated whip in the world, is as well known in New York's Madison Square Garden and at the Royal Winter Fair in Toronto as she is at the Royal International and Horse of the Year shows. She and her husband have the best breeding stock in the world at their home in the Cotswolds and breed world champions with almost monotonous regularity. Cynthia Haydon had also competed with Hackneys in several world and European combined driving championships.

Hunter-bred mares and geldings have long been exportable

commodities to the United States and Canada, both as hunters and, more recently, to compete in world-class three-day events or horse trials. The Canadian team which won the world championship in Lexington, Kentucky, in 1978 was largely composed of British-bred horses supplied as youngsters by the triple Badminton winner, Sheila Willcox. No fewer than four were English-bred, as well as two of the American team horses and one, Power Games by Game Rights (a premium stallion), of the German team which finished third.

English show ponies have always had a small vogue in the United States and Canada, where they are made to go on a loose rein and poke their noses, the antithesis of the way they are produced in England. These are the real blue-bloods of the pony world, with beautiful heads, small, quality ears, exquisite large eyes, lovely light, floating action and very high courage. Side-saddle ponies come into the same category, slightly longer in the body but with great quality and impeccable manners. Mrs David Barham of Bury St Edmunds took over to the Equitaner exhibition in Essen, West Germany, an entire side-saddle display. Both ponies and riders were warmly appreciated and returned in 1987, their first visit having been in 1985.

They commenced with ten and finished with twelve, and started training in November, leaving on 9 March with working hunter types, ranging from 13 to 15hh bays and greys which would carry a side-saddle well, with a leg at each corner. They were accompanied by six stewards, concerned with wardrobe, press and publicity, and six grooms. All were the guests of Equitaner Essen and the hospitality was wonderful. The first stop was at Herning in Denmark for the stallion show, where they had a very happy time, and then after a long drive they reached Essen, where the hospitality was over-whelming. The trip was made possible by their sponsors, who were 'real fairy godmothers'. Lambourn Horse Boxes not only transported them all the way for nothing but were rewarded by orders. The Regency ride went down extremely well with a total crowd of 200,000.

Mrs M. E. Mansfield, who visits Australia and New Zealand regularly to judge at their major shows and has exported many Welsh and riding ponies there of her own breeding from her Rotherwood Stud at Ashby-de-la-Zouch, answered the telephone while holding a stallion which was waiting to cover a mare. The girl holding the mare had the foresight not to bring the mare into his line of vision, or his welcoming whinnies would have precluded any exchange of conversation. As it was, I rang again. Australians, she confirmed, are extremely keen on English riding and native ponies from the UK, their breeding societies are very enthusiastic, all the children belong to the Pony Club and in every town and village the local Pony Club centre is signposted as prominently as the village hall might be over here. It is a horse-mad country, as is New Zealand, the children are very interested and are really ravenous for horsey books, which sell like hot cakes when they get over there. She had tried to find some good pony books which would explain the points of our nine native breeds and the riding ponies and working hunter ponies, but there is a dearth of such publications worldwide. In particular, they are desperate in New South Wales, West Australia and New Zealand for such books, but it seems that they are no longer published.

Mrs Mansfield left for Australia on 1 February, the height of their show season, to attend the Victoria All-Welsh Show – principally a breeders' show – and the Victoria Pony of the Year Show at Barastoc. There were many imported ponies which she met up with again, and now that the years have gone by since the first ones went out, a large amount of stock has been bred up from them. 'It is lovely, and rewarding,' she said, 'to see a sort of evolution of the English-type riding pony taking place.'

The Welsh Pony Society reported a record export year in 1978, when of the 2,158 ponies to leave these shores, 75 for West Germany and 90 for France were included. Now exported ponies average from 187 to 200, and besides Germany and France they go to the United States, Denmark, Spain, Belgium, Canada, South Africa and Australia and Holland. Some 4,000 ponies – 2,400 fillies, 1,100 colts and 500 geldings – are registered each year.

The diminutive Dartmoor pony is an easy second to the Welsh in the export stakes. Boveycombe Buckthorn, bred at Lustleigh by Mrs M. J. Gould, is ruling the roost in Australia, while in the United States, where Mrs Romaine has an old-established Dartmoor stud in Virginia, Shilstone Rocks Hannibal, bred near Widecombe by Mrs Reep, holds court. Three years ago Bronley Jack Frost arrived in the USA as a further boost for the breed, which enjoys great popularity both as children's ponies and for driving in harness competitions. Holland is another country where the Dartmoor goes down well – they can boast a driven team of five geldings.

There are also Dartmoors on the Falkland Islands (they were part of the Noah's Ark scheme), in particular Shilstone Rocks Forest Fury, while in Sweden a Swedish Dartmoor Pony Society is taking off after a slow start. Norway is also enthusiastic about the breed, and there are many registered ponies in France, whence they are interchanged with West Germany and Holland fairly regularly. There are a large number in Denmark, where good stock has been sent and they are regarded as the pony for all generations; I learnt from the lively secretary, Mrs Williamson of Weston Manor, Corscombe, Dorset, that when a child has outgrown their Dartmoor, mother or even grandmother will start to drive it.

Eleven Exmoor ponies were included in the Noah's Ark trip to the Falklands, and three or four have gone to California. They are popular in Norway, Denmark and Canada, both as driving ponies and for long-distance riding, and they are being bred in Holland and Germany too, for four-in-hand driving competitions at international fixtures.

The Connemara pony is famed far beyond its native Ireland, and rightly so, for not only are they ideal mounts for children and light adults in the hunting field, but they are also, crossed with the Thoroughbred, international show-jumpers (like Tommy Wade's lion-hearted Dundrum) and dressage horses (like Mrs V. D. S. Williams' Little Model, who reached Olympic standard). They are also wonderful foundation stock for almost every type of riding animal. They are tremendously popular in the United States and Canada, as well as Australia, and have been for many years, while they are also found in large numbers in France, Switzerland, Italy, Germany, Finland and Belgium. In their native habitat they are said to subsist on 'bracken and bog-water' and although this is overstating their case, they are extremely hardy and well able to survive on very sparse herbage.

In the Sixties and Seventies there was an export explosion to the United States, Sweden, Denmark, Holland, Germany, France, Finland, Australia and New Zealand. Now all of these countries have their own Connemara Pony Societies and they are breeding their own stock, but they continue to come back to Connemara for new blood. The export trade was badly hit by the oil crisis of 1973. Previously, it cost £18 a head to export a pony to the Continent through Rotterdam, but now the cost is £400–£500, while to export to Australia is quite prohibitive, around £4,000 per pony.

USEFUL ADDRESSES

Arab Horse Society
C. C. Pearson, Goddards Green, Cranbrook, Kent TN17 3LP

British Horse Society
C. Smith, British Equestrian Centre, Stoneleigh, Kenilworth, Warwickshire CV8 2LG

British Show Pony Society
Mrs J. Toynton, 124 Green End Road, Sawtry, Huntingdon, Cambs

Cleveland Bay Society
J. F. Stephenson, York Livestock Centre, Murton, York YO1 3UF

Dales Pony Society
Miss P. A. Fitzgerald, 55 Cromwell Street, Walkley, Sheffield S6 3RN

Dartmoor Pony Society
Mrs E. C. Williamson, Weston Manor, Corscombe, Dorset DT12 0PB

English Connemara Pony Society
Mrs M. V. Newman, 2 The Leys, Salford, Chipping Norton, Oxon OX7 5FD

Exmoor Pony Society
D. Mansell, Glen Fern, Waddicombe, Dulverton, Somerset TA22 9R7

Fell Pony Society
C. Richardson, 19 Dragley Beck, Ulverston, Cumbria

Hackney Horse Society
Miss S. Oliver, 34 Stockton, Warminster, Wiltshire

Highland Pony Society
Mrs S. Bell, Orwell House, Milnathort, Kinross-shire KY13 7YQ

Hunters' Improvement Society (National Light Horse Breeding Society)
G. G. Evans, 96 High Street, Edenbridge, Kent TN8 5AR

Irish Draught Horse Society (GB)
J. Wood-Roberts, 4th Street, National Agricultural Centre, Stoneleigh, Kenilworth, Warwickshire CV8 2LG

National Pony Society
Colonel A. R. Whent, Brook House, 25 High Street, Alton, Hants GU34 1AW

New Forest Pony Breeding Society
Miss D. Macnair, Beacon Corner, Burley, Ringwood, Hants BH24 4EW

Shetland Pony Stud Book Society
D. M. Patterson, 8 Whinfield Road, Montrose, Angus DD10 8SA

Thoroughbred Breeders Association
S. G. Sheppard, Stanstead House, The Avenue, Newmarket, Suffolk CB8 9AA

Welsh Pony and Cob Society
T. E. Roberts, 6 Chalybeate Street, Aberystwyth, Dyfed SY23 1HS

INDEX